The Art of Heraldry

Origins • Symbols • Designs

The Art of
Heraldry

Origins • Symbols • Designs

Peter Gwynn-Jones
Garter King of Arms

PROSPERO
B·O·O·K·S
A DIVISION OF CHAPTERS INC.

First Published in Great Britain in 1998
by Parkgate Books Ltd, Kiln House,
210 New King's Road, London SW6 4NZ

This edition produced for Prospero Books,
a division of Chapters Inc.

British Library Cataloguing in Publication
Data: A CIP catalogue record for this book
is available from the British Library.

ISBN 1 894102 34 7

Printed and bound in Singapore

Acknowledgements

Acknowledgements to my secretaries Jennifer
Long and Jill Garrod, the latter for initiating
the typing of the text and the former for
continuing and retyping the whole and
comprehending my voice on the tape. To my
colleague Thomas Woodcock, Norroy and
Ulster King of Arms, for vetting the text with
constructive comments. To my colleague
David White, Rouge Croix Pursuivant, for
joining with me on forays into nineteenth-
century heraldry. To Gillian Barlow for her
colour drawings and whose decorative
borders to letters patent are a major feature
of this book. I am also indebted to Gillian
Barlow for her help in picture research. To
Henrietta Webb for her colour drawings, for
reading the text and providing needed
punctuation marks. To Sally Acloque for
reading the text with useful comments. To
Robert Yorke, the archivist of the College of
Arms, for finding appropriate grants of arms.
To Julia Hett for her help in collating the
illustrations and for general assistance. To the
Chapter of the College of Arms for its support
and for its permission to use illustrations
from its official records. To Jacqueline Rose
and Tim Noad whose work is also illustrated
and to Robert Parsons, Dennis Field and
Henry Gray whose help and guidance on the
art of heraldry over the years have been
invaluable. The work of Jacqueline Rose is
demonstrated by the patent of arms to Hicks
and the painting for Rose with its chameleon
supporters. The work of Tim Noad is found
with the patent to Howell, and Robert
Parsons painted the armorial bearings of
Solpro which feature on the front cover.

CONTENTS

Introduction

THERE HAVE BEEN many books on heraldry. Most have followed in the tradition of medieval heraldic treatises, listing charges or devices, outlining accepted principles of blazon or description and setting out the finer points of heraldic practice. As guides or textbooks they are invaluable to any reader with a dedicated interest in the subject; but in concentrating on the science of heraldry, they have overlooked its artistic nature. References to the different styles of different periods and to the heralds and designers are largely absent. It is this neglect which this book seeks to redress. It is, after all, the visual impact of heraldry which can be enjoyed for itself without any need for knowledge of its somewhat esoteric technology.

The textbook approach with its emphasis on rules and regulations encourages the belief that heraldry is essentially a medieval leftover. This is understandable considering that the main corpus of heraldic principles was established in the Middle Ages; but it is a misguided belief. Although heraldry may have a medieval origin, it must not be forgotten that the early Tudor period was far more imaginative and exuberant in heraldic design than anything found in previous centuries. This was largely the responsibility of Sir Thomas Wriothesley, whose name goes unmentioned in most books on the subject.

Following Wriothesley there have been other 'schools' and 'periods' of heraldic art, each with their own characteristic style; and in the late twentieth century heraldry is still alive, creative and flourishing. This book seeks to treat with these different styles and to bring the reader up to date. That it is illustrated with an emphasis on post-medieval and particularly current heraldry is therefore deliberate. Although it is clearly desirable that the great tradition of heraldry should be enjoyed, the building on that tradition is also essential, for no art form can gainfully remain static, tied forever to the past.

The inclusion of much twentieth-century heraldry in this book provides a welcome opportunity to show something of the skill of the herald painter, whose interpretation of heraldry and the artistic decoration of letters patent, the documents whereby grants of armorial bearings are made, has too often gone unrecognised. To this dedicated body of men and women, the art of heraldry owes an incalculable debt.

In the creation of new designs, use has always been made of the geometric, based on the original formations established from the beginning of heraldry in the twelfth century. Like musical notes they can be treated to endless permutations and artistic combinations. As such they form puns on names or allusions to occupations and interests. They are also arguably more satisfactory than man-made inanimate objects. Too often the latter seem incongruous or rapidly become outdated. Whilst a castle or a sword has acquired a measure of tradition, and hence a timeless quality, a telephone or a car has not. A lion issuing from the turrets of a castle or a lion grasping a sword is acceptable, but a lion sitting in an open jeep or a lion holding a telephone suggests a debased form of heraldry. Telecommunication and motorised transport are better represented by a more subtle use of geometric form. Perhaps the future will reject this and see in contemporary man-made objects scope for its own particular 'school' of heraldic design.

In addition to the geometric, heraldry has drawn heavily on flora and fauna, with species continuing to make their first appearance in heraldic design. Artistic treatment has often led to an evolved form of fanciful creature or plant far removed from its natural origin which in the process has become obscure or forgotten. In seeking to reveal this origin a book of limited scope can only take a few species and follow what suggests itself as the most obvious line of evolution. This is bound to leave unanswered questions and courts a measure of controversy. There may be some, for example, who point to the presence of more than one type of unicorn in the bestiaries or medieval books of beasts. Others may suggest a possible Muslim influence on heraldry by drawing attention to the recurring appearance of what seems to be a fleur-de-lys in Muslim decoration. These and other questions must here remain unaddressed, for the limitations imposed on this book make it necessary to stay on what has been considered the main track. If, by following this track through the thickets of artistic interpretation and evolution, some controversial turns have been taken, this is perhaps no bad thing. Debate on the origins of material used in heraldry will be a refreshing diversion from the repetition of heraldic technology.

That heraldry in one of its aspects should be seen as an art form is appropriate, for its very origin coincides with the twelfth-century Renaissance with its emphasis on decoration. This book suggests that it was the love of the visual, so characteristic of the period, which was a major factor in that origin. Art was an integral part of heraldry at its inception, it has always been there and today it continues to provide visual enjoyment. Something of this will, it is hoped, be conveyed in the following pages. For those anxious that the science of heraldry should not be completely brushed aside, a brief and rudimentary glossary is included.

chapter 1

A History of
Heraldry

From the Bayeux Tapestry to the Present Day

Left: Shields of knights depicted on the Bayeux Tapestry featured dragon-like formations similar to those used as decorative infillings on English heraldic seals circa 1300. Others bore wavy geometric designs, which have never been satisfactorily explained.

Below: The genealogical tree bearing the arms of the Bavarian family of Ströhl from the early seventeenth century, illustrated in Herr Ströhl's *Heraldischer Atlas*.

THE GENERALLY ACCEPTED definition of heraldry is the hereditary use of a systematic arrangement of charges or devices centred on a shield. In spite of many forceful and categorical arguments, the exact nature and purpose of its origin remain obscure.

A landmark in the chronicling of heraldry was made at the turn of the century by H.G. Ströhl, the celebrated German heraldic artist. Completed in 1899, his sumptuous *Heraldischer Atlas* far surpassed any previous heraldic publication, and attracted great attention. It chiefly consisted of carefully chosen and representative examples of heraldic art from its inception, selected from the whole of Europe. Although Ströhl's emphasis naturally fell on the heraldry of his own country, he was obliged to reflect on historic sources from regions throughout the continent which long predated modern political borders.

The Bayeux Tapestry recording the Norman invasion of England in 1066 must be taken into account in any study of early heraldry. The tapestry depicts knights bearing shields decorated

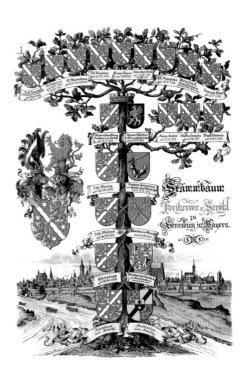

11

with wavy geometrical designs and dragon-like creatures. It also shows some thirty or more lance flags variously decorated. It has been argued that these lance devices were already hereditary and can be traced back to the early ninth-century empire of Charlemagne. It is then asserted that descendants of Charlemagne's magnates were allied with William the Conqueror at Hastings and that their lance devices were ultimately transferred to the shields of their immediate descendants; unfortunately, little positive evidence has been forthcoming to support this intriguing theory. Nonetheless, of these lance flags, one appears to show three buckles which were later borne on the shield of the Malet family; and William Malet is known to have been at the Battle of Hastings. He remains the only known participant in the battle who is considered a likely candidate for having male line descendants living today. Others have argued that the decorations on the Bayeux Tapestry shields in themselves constituted heraldry, in spite of the fact that these types of decoration are not found in early seals or rolls of arms and must therefore have lacked any hereditary element.

The Bayeux Tapestry may be misleading. The observant Princess Anna Comnena of Byzantium describes in her diary the shield borne by the Frankish knights taking part in the First Crusade in 1096. It was extremely smooth and gleaming with a brilliant boss of molten brass. There is no mention of anything on the surface of the shield suggestive of personal or hereditary devices. Clearly, it is difficult to reconcile the shields depicted in the Bayeux Tapestry with Anna Comnena's eye-witness account. It seems unlikely that

Above: The seal of John de Kingeston; from the Barons' letter to the Pope, 1301, showing wyverns, or two-legged dragons, similar to those found in the Bayeux Tapestry.
COLL. ARMS VINCENT COLLECTION

Right: The seal of Ralph de Monthermer, Earl of Gloucester and Hereford; from the Barons' letter, 1301, which contains ninety-six such shields. Approximately one-third of these are set between pairs of similar wyverns, which suggests that these were decorative and not particular to individuals. Hence they lacked any heraldic significance.
COLL. ARMS VINCENT COLLECTION

the style and nature of the shields of Western European knights would have altered so dramatically within thirty years.

Recently, certain details included in the Bayeux Tapestry have given rise to a degree of scepticism. Attention has been drawn to the condition of the tapestry and features of the work relating to eating habits and dress which all point to a much later origin. There is a growing school of thought that successive custodians of the tapestry may have effected doodles and infillings; but until its threads are subjected to scientific examination, doubts must remain unresolved. Given the possibility of later infillings, however, the shield decorations should be treated with a measure of caution. Certainly, the indeterminate dragon formations found on the shields bear close similarity to the dragon-like decorations found as infillings on the seals of Edward I's barons signing their letter to the Pope in 1301.

Anna Comnena's description of plain shields with polished bosses would conform with the general belief that early twelfth-century shields were wooden and covered on both sides with leather, to which extra defences of metal were added. It is also known that from the late eleventh century to the beginning of the thirteenth century the elongated shield became progressively shorter. This reduction in size and hence weight allowed for a greater strengthening of the remaining surface. Further metallic pieces, such as studs and bands, could then be added. It is this restructuring of the shield that is likely to have played a major part in the formation of early heraldry, the metal additions encouraging painted decoration.

Writing in about 1170, Jean of Marmoutier in his history of Anjou describes how, in 1127, King Henry I invested his son-in-law, Geoffrey Plantagenet, with a blue shield charged with little lions of gold. This is generally accepted as the first known instance of recorded heraldry. Although Jean of Marmoutier's writings have been described as 'lively and often apocryphal', Geoffrey's enamel tomb plate at Le Mans Cathedral shows precisely such a shield. Geoffrey died in 1151; and his grandson, William Longespee, Earl of Salisbury, who died in 1226, has the identical shield on his tomb in Salisbury Cathedral. Geoffrey's shield had acquired a significance that enabled it to become hereditary.

The enamel plate on the tomb of Geoffrey Plantagenet at Le Mans. He died in 1151 and his shield of arms is generally regarded as the earliest recorded example of heraldry in Europe. MUSÉE TESSÉ, LE MANS, FRANCE

Opposite page: Top: The arms of the Aufenstein family incorporate Or, standing on a stone (*stein*) sable, and an owl (*auf*). The family originally came from Tyrol, but later owned large estates in Kärnten.
Centre: Arms of the Capodilista family of Padua, an early example (1435) of Italian heraldry.
Bottom: Arms of the Nicolay family, domiciled in the Isle de France and Vivaris, taken from a heraldic book of the Chambre de Comptes (1768).

Below: Arms of the Holy Roman-German Emperor (1446).

Unfortunately, the actual accoutrements of war and in particular shields have not survived from the twelfth century. Evidence for any heraldry existing at that time is largely dependent upon seals. A number of extant seals dating from the second or third quarters of the twelfth century depict devices on shields that were subsequently adopted by descendants of the first user. This early evidence of heraldry on seals suggests that the purpose of heraldry was not necessarily the identification of combatants in battle, as many have supposed.

It is apparent that much of the science and system of heraldry developed as part of European rather than national culture. Common ground and personal contact were established between the knights of Europe through their affiliation to the Latin church and found a practical outlet in the Crusades. However, the ideals of chivalry may not have carried the overwhelming impetus in heraldic development that many would wish. Chivalry existed alongside extreme brutality; and heraldry was adopted by the practitioners of both within the overall European context. There remained characteristics peculiar to different countries or groups of countries. In Eastern Europe, whole groups of families or territorial areas adopted the same armorial bearings, a form of clan affiliation unknown elsewhere. France and the British Isles were foremost in applying marks of difference to the shield to distinguish between several members or branches of the same family: further east, this practice is usually absent. German or Teutonic heraldry extended its sphere of influence over Central Europe and spread northwards into Scandinavia.

Although the presence of heraldic insignia on shields has inevitably linked the origins of European heraldry and its widespread adoption with warfare, a consideration of the nature of the twelfth-century battlefield will cast doubt on the likelihood of identification in battle as being the impulse behind its evolution. Medieval battles were generally ill-planned. The users of heraldry, that is to say the barons and knights, did not arrange themselves in tactical order. The sole exception to this was the Order of the Templars in Europe, where a rule emphasised that no brother of the Order was to attack on his own initiative or move beyond the general formation. Otherwise there seems to have been a general mounted charge of one side against the other. Certainly this was very different from the regimented operations of cavalry warfare of post-medieval Europe. Although it may have allowed for some individual combat after the initial charge, the identification of a specific opponent by means of heraldic devices must remain in doubt.

The surface of the medieval shield was essentially two-dimensional and could only be viewed from a limited angle. Furthermore, it was borne on the general level of the battlefield and rapidly acquired mud, scratches and other battle filth. These difficulties in obtaining a clear view and identifying a besmirched two-dimensional surface borne at body height in the medieval charge and any subsequent melee would have been further compounded by the nature of the devices used. An examination of early rolls of arms will show considerable similarity between overall designs and repetition of the limited number of devices used. The thirteenth-century *Heralds' Roll*, for example, consists of 195 shields, of which no fewer than 43 contain the lion. Even if a would-be antagonist had gone to the lengths of apprising himself of his opponent's heraldry, it is unlikely that he would have been able to recognise his opponent's arms with any degree of certainty on the battlefield.

At this time a system of heraldry was also developing in Japan. It was to feature on the Japanese battlefield long after medieval warfare had ceased in Europe. Although it is totally uninfluenced by Western Europe, there are remarkable similarities. Equivalent to European knights were the samurai, each having their own individual device, or *mon*, which was fiercely protected and governed by strict rules and regulations. The shoguns and military warlords used their armorial devices on field curtains and rallying banners. These were well known by all participants in any battle. In contrast the individual samurai bore his own device on small roundels on his armour, which could not have been identified until a close inspection was made after his death. The delight-

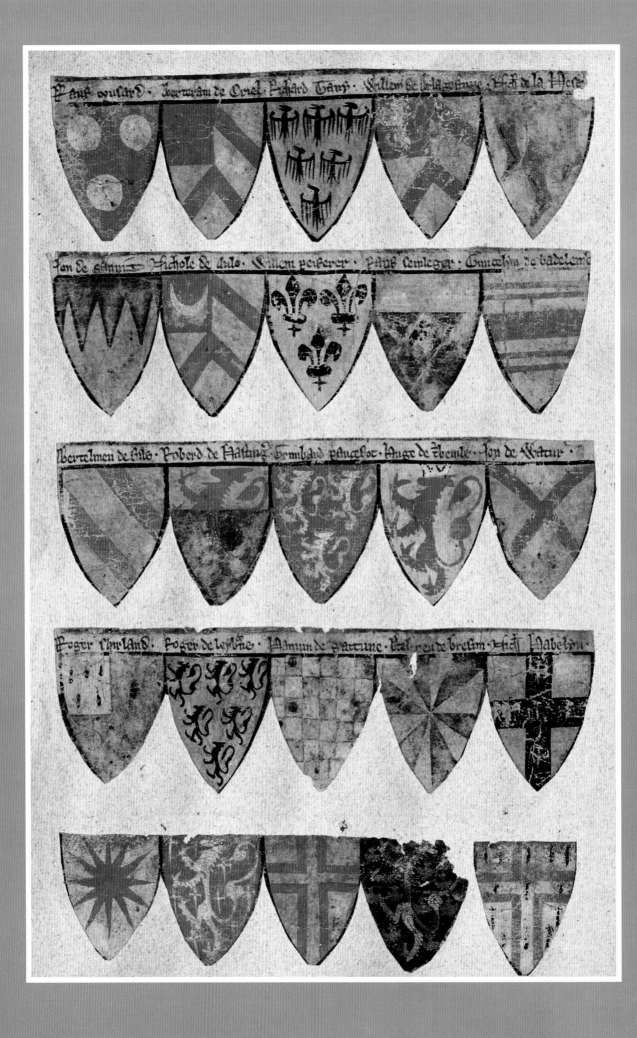

ful and subtle designs of individual samurai *mon* were of great personal importance and an integral part of Japanese civilisation. They were readily identified on seals and personal possessions; but their use on small roundels in the battlefield was minimal and lacking in practical purpose. With a type of warfare not dissimilar to medieval Europe, together with a developed system of heraldry, the Japanese experience may shed light on its medieval European counterpart. There is no doubt that the arms of the three lions of England and the arms of well-known baronial magnates were generally recognised and may have been used as flags and rallying points in the medieval battlefield. However, the arms of individual knights bearing similar devices remained unrecognised by both friend and foe alike. It is arguable that had individual knights raised their arms on battlefield flags, greater confusion would have occurred and such proliferation and display of similar devices would have been strongly discouraged, if not actively penalised. Too many lions apparent on the battlefield might have incurred the wrath of the Plantagenet with his own lions, whereas their discreet use in a less flamboyant fashion was perfectly acceptable.

During a period characterised equally by chivalry and brutishness, when there was an emphasis on the civilian use of heraldry manifested in seals and identification in battle was largely impractical, some other factor must have existed to explain the sudden and spontaneous appearance of heraldry. In this respect, it is significant that the beginning of heraldry in the twelfth century coincides exactly with an explosive advance made by European civilisation, now known as the twelfth-century Renaissance. This movement was characterised by an exuberance of spirit and self-confidence which was primarily manifested in a delight of visual decoration. This found an obvious outlet on the personal shield of the knight, with its newly developed structural changes incorporating

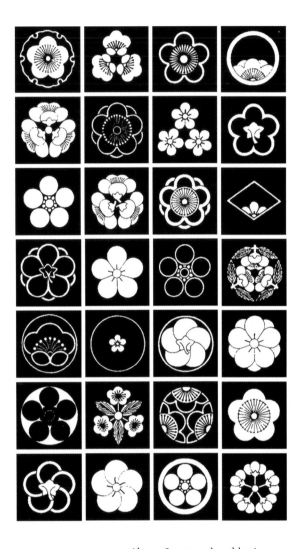

Above: Japanese heraldry in the form of *mon*. Small and intricate designs particular to the individual would have made heraldic identification on the battlefield impractical. Only the more important *mon* of the military leaders were made conspicuous on banners and field curtains.

Opposite page: Early arms in the *Heralds' Roll*, painted circa 1270-1280.
COLL. ARMS HERALDS' ROLL F 26B

17

Lions in medieval arms painted circa 1380 in *Jenyns' Ordinary*. Although each shield is different, their similarity would have been confusing on the battlefield. Coll. Arms Jenyns' Ordinary ff 5b

bosses and bands of metal or leather. It is perhaps with this spirit rather than with military tactics that the real origin of heraldry should be sought.

Once decorated, shields became the objects of personal pride. As such, like the Japanese samurai, there was a great element of the subjective manifested by the wish to have a personal device similar to a modern mascot, rather than any positive desire to provide an objective means of personal identification on the battlefield. Such devices could be recognised on smaller items such as seals where they fulfilled the place of a modern signature. Undoubtedly the adoption of heraldry was further stimulated by the tournament, but here again pomp and pageantry were subjective

18

A Wolmershausen and Rhenish knight in individual combat in 1471. They display the customary array of heraldic insignia worn at tournament in the fifteenth century. The pageantry of tournament served to stimulate the development of European heraldry.

rather than practical. As the Middle Ages proceeded, the tournament developed from a rough and ready melee of teams of knights ranging over wide tracts of countryside, to highly organised lists where individual knights were pitted against each other with a great display of personal heraldic insignia. These included crests, which first made their appearance in the thirteenth century and consisted of three-dimensional objects made out of wood or boiled leather strapped or buckled on to the top of the helm. Supporters appeared in the fourteenth century. They are now shown as animals or human figures standing on either side of the shield and supporting it. However, in the fifteenth century, there is some evidence to suggest that they were animated; and pageboys may have been dressed up as heraldic creatures holding their lord's shield in the pageantry surrounding the tournament. Their origin is to be sought in those devices found in seals in the thirteenth century in the form of decorative infilling between the side of the shield and the edge of the seal. There was considerable duplication in this decoration, with repetitious lions, the wingless dragon of the Bayeux Tapestry and the occasional inclusion of foliage, suggesting that these infillings were largely decorative with little heraldic significance. It was not until the end of the fourteenth or even the beginning of the fifteenth century that they began to acquire that significance, and pairs of supporters distinctive to a particular individual became apparent.

Such display associated with the tournament is a far cry from the heraldry that had filtered through society from the twelfth century onwards, so that by the end of the fifteenth century most villages in this country had their 'knight' or gentleman bearing for civilian use a shield of arms. The term 'knight' derives from his feudal land-owning in return for knight service which had long since been exchanged by his ancestors for scutage or payment to the crown. Tournament pageantry was of no concern to the gentleman of the typical English village. It is this civilian use of heraldry that prevented its decline or disappearance with the cessation of medieval warfare at the end of the fifteenth century. On the contrary, the Battle of Bosworth in 1485 and the start of the Tudor period ushered in perhaps the richest and most creative period of English heraldry. The tournament class in contrast remained limited to a courtly circle where personal pomp and display encouraged the use of crests and supporters, accessories unused by the main body of the heraldic section of society.

Below: Crest of a horse's head on the Garter stall plate of Sir Walter Paveley who died in 1375. Horses are rarely found in medieval heraldry. The horse was essentially a subservient animal, a quality which had little appeal.
THE KNIGHTS OF THE ORDER OF THE GARTER, ST JOHN HOPE, VI

Right : Crests painted in the early sixteenth century, but mainly of medieval origin.
COLL. ARMS VINCENT 152 F 77

This divergence between arms rendered on seals and, by the end of the Middle Ages, on many items of personal use, and the real physical shield borne by tournament participants with accompanying crests and supporters was recognised by the early Tudor heralds. They brought the crest across this divide with the kings of arms issuing letters patent confirming existing arms and granting new crests. Thereafter any new grant of armorial bearings has invariably included both arms and crest. This decision of the Tudor heralds was farsighted, as today it is invariably the crest which is borne on signet rings and the like whilst the owner is too often ignorant of the nature of his shield of arms. On the other hand, supporters remained restricted and in the twentieth century they are still confined to peers of the realm, knights grand cross of the several orders of knighthood and the more prestigious corporate bodies.

Of greater practical military importance was the badge. This was a free-standing device adopted by the medieval magnate during the fourteenth and fifteenth centuries. It was borne by the followers and retainers of those capable of sustaining sizeable levies of men. As such the badge became much better known than individual arms and in consequence played a significant part in battlefield identification. It was similar to the flags and banners raised by the limited number of major contestants on the medieval battlefield. It is significant that even the well-known badges of such contestants could become confused. At the Battle of Barnet in 1471, the Earl of Warwick confused the silver star or mullet of the Earl of Oxford with the white Yorkist rose, attacked his own supporters and lost the day.

If a well-known badge displayed by a large body of men proved confusing on the battlefield, it clearly emphasises that the personal heraldic devices of the mass of individuals had limited or no practical purpose.

The decision to revive the badge was taken in 1906 by Sir Alfred Scott-Gatty, Garter King of Arms, and may prove to be as important in the development of heraldry as the decision to grant crests by the Tudor heralds. As with medieval usage the badge today is not confined to the grantee of arms and male line descendants. It may be borne by other associated bodies or individuals, and is

Arms, crest and supporters of King Henry VI and King Edward IV. Additional badges are shown on banners.
COLL. ARMS VINCENT 152 F 53.

Medieval badges frequently derived from arms or crest; here, badges are painted on the left of crests, circa 1460.
Coll. Arms MS M3 f 39

particularly useful for otherwise non-armigerous sons-in-law and grandchildren in the female line, who may therefore be seen as the modern successors of baronial followers and retainers.

Scott-Gatty was only one of many heralds whose names and biographies stretch back into the Middle Ages. How and when heralds became linked with heraldry is once again a subject of speculation. Early references to heralds date from the twelfth century and are invariably connected with the tournament. The first generally accepted reference to a herald dates from about 1170 when Chrétien de Troyes writes of a barefoot herald clad only in a shirt running to identify the arms of Lancelot in an Arthurian legend. This he fails to do. It is salutary that the first record of a herald is his failure to recognise a shield of arms. Nonetheless, this twelfth-century reference, the precursor of many from the same period, shows that heralds were concerned with armorial bearings. Their connection with tournaments meant that they were involved with the pageantry and the announcing of knights entering the jousting lists, and this in turn led them to becoming masters of ceremony. To what extent they were the designers of early heraldry is unknown. There is nothing to suggest that the painting of early twelfth-century shields by individual knights was subject to any central control or designing authority. However, by 1300 heraldic treatises were coming into existence. The earliest, *De Heraudie*, of unknown authorship, provides evidence of armorial blazon or description, a practice and accepted convention that must therefore have developed previously. The authorship of many of these treatises is obscure; but it seems likely that the heralds were deeply involved and probably responsible for establishing the rules and regulations. They may indeed constitute the common source that has meant that the art of heraldry is consistent during any particular medieval period over large areas of western Europe.

Later European regional differences tended to become more emphasised as medieval civilization gave way to the growth of nationalism and the evolution of strong centralised monarchies which took upon themselves the control of armorial bearings and appointed their own heraldic authorities. Holland and Switzerland stood unrivalled in their widespread use of heraldry. Holland in particular is notable for the great esteem with which Dutch families regard their armorial bearings. Many old medieval families, if not extinguished by the Wars of Independence, fled to the Spanish Netherlands (modern Belgium) and their place was taken by republican traders and merchants who themselves began an extensive adoption of arms. Burgher arms that date from the late Middle Ages, when the Low Countries became Europe's commercial and industrial centre, are characterised by the absence of helmets.

The heraldry of Italy reflects its troubled history: successive German, French, Spanish and Austrian invaders all left their mark. But despite foreign intervention, Italian heraldry has developed certain characteristics distinctive to itself, in particular the use of almond-shaped or horsehead-shaped shields. The rise of the northern city states and the general fragmentation of the country led to certain duplication of armorial bearings. Central Italian heraldry has been much influenced by the church. Many families who derived their titles from successive popes have alluded to this by incorporating papal insignia in their arms, most notably the papal tiara and the crossed keys.

Above: Arms of Specht von Bubenheim (Rhineland), and the Counts of Nassau. Below: Arms of the Torricelli, who belonged to the ancient nobility of Upper Italy. Horsehead-shaped shields such as this were characteristic of Italian heraldry.

Hungarian heraldry is closely akin to that of Austria and Germany, but differs in two particular respects. First, there is a marked preference for devices associated with the Turkish wars, a perennial feature of Hungarian history from the fifteenth to the eighteenth centuries. The second characteristic is the occasional extravagance typified by the arms of the Hajduboszormeny, charged with a firing gun, beneath which are burning logs and above a friendly sun, the whole encircled by a green dragon bearing a patriarchal cross. Poland separates itself from the rest of Europe by virtue of the pre-heraldic runic signs which were later absorbed by heraldry and came to constitute its principal feature.

In France, the revolution of 1789 saw the abolition of heraldry, which was replaced some fifteen years later by a new imperial heraldry. This was predictably characterised by weapons and items of war reflecting Napoleonic campaigns. Specific charges and arrangements of design were also laid down for several grades of

the nobility and officials, and were even extended to civic heraldry. In this last class, the chief or canton was often charged with the symbols favoured by Napoleon such as the initial 'N', the Imperial crown and bees.

In England, the Crown had gradually assumed to itself the right to grant, confirm and regulate all armorial bearings by the end of the fourteenth century. Thereafter it delegated that power to the kings of arms, the senior grade of its own personal heralds. This situation continues today and has meant that all new heraldry coming into existence since the beginning of the fifteenth century has been the responsibility of the kings of arms or the heralds and pursuivants acting as their agents. In colloquial use the term 'herald' has been applied to embrace all these three grades of the profession.

The Crown delegation for heraldic responsibility at the end of the fourteenth century breaks through the anonymity of design. Heralds, and particularly the kings of arms, can be identified with the particular coat of arms that they granted, and judged responsible for the changing style and art form of heraldry over the subsequent centuries. The art of heraldry has therefore depended upon the heralds as designers.

The intention of subsequent chapters is to examine something of the raw material used by the heralds in their designing, their changes in taste over the centuries and the reason for their choice of devices or charges. Heralds have drawn upon the traditions of heraldry, but within those traditions there is huge scope for new and imaginative designs, tapping in particular the geometric formations of the Middle Ages which have so frequently been borrowed from heraldry and turned into many successful modern logos and trade marks. Beyond the geometric, there is the natural world, not only its flora and fauna, which heraldry has used from its inception, but also the monstrous, which it has evolved and made particular to itself. Heraldry has also dabbled with the inanimate; but few inanimate charges have stood the test of time. However slow in physical terms it may be, the arrow formation has acquired and still retains the timeless quality of speed; similarly the castle exemplifies qualities of strength and fortitude. Unfortunately, other man-made objects too soon become obsolete and are probably better distilled and presented in allusive and

Opposite page: Quarterings shown on the arms of Sir John Grey of Ruthin who died in 1439. Quartering or the system of marshalling different arms together on a single shield to denote marriages to heraldic heiresses is believed to have been introduced into England by Eleanor of Castile, the wife of King Edward I.
THE KNIGHTS OF THE ORDER OF THE GARTER, ST JOHN HOPE, LIV

Above: Arms of Jean Domenique, whom Napoleon created Baron Larry in 1810. Inspector-General of the Military Medicinal Staff, he was one of the greatest surgeons of his time, and served as such in Napoleon's army.

84 Woupiſſou ·   kyrkeby ·   Bentle ·   Corbet aſton ·   Burus

85 Elliſworthe ·   zork ·   Judde ·   Arnyn ·

86 Beaufiz ·   Tybbis ·   Oſanne ·

87 Tyttiſbury ·   Bahon ·   Engayn ·   Bynley ·   Medes

188 Harſale ·   Montſhaunt ·   Hargoſt ·   Boynton ·   Suytayo ·

26

geometric formation or symbolised by something out of the natural world. This is not to close the door on the inanimate. On the contrary, it has vast scope for future heraldic design and this should be harnessed, but it needs a certain filtering to acquire, for example, the timelessness of the arrow in order to ensure permanency, which is the essence of heraldry.

The founding of the English College of Arms in 1484 and the retention of an heraldic authority under the Crown have been of immeasurable significance in the art of British heraldry, to which the granting of armorial bearings by successive Lyon Kings of Arms in Scotland has also contributed. This has ensured a long and rich heraldic culture that the assiduous research and superb illustrations offered by Herr Ströhl in his *Heraldischer Atlas* were unable fully to embrace. Whereas heraldic authorities have been generally swept away in continental Europe with the political upheavals of the last two centuries, the English Kings of Arms have continued to grant new armorial bearings, and heraldry beyond Europe has been much influenced by the English.

For centuries arms had always been the possession of the higher feudal castes and indirectly served as marks of social distinction for the bearer; yet English heraldry prevailed in North America despite republican hostilites to the hierarchy it represented, and continues to have influence in the New World. Nowadays heraldry no longer has a military or caste connotation but still denotes distinction of groups or institutions. British expansion overseas and the vast extent of the old empire stretched and tested the heraldic authorities, bringing a resurgence in the understanding and significance of symbols and devices, as well as enriching the artistic boundaries of heraldry. It is the branch of English heraldry, therefore, more than its European counterpart, that bears the most fruitful study for the modern scholar and enthusiast.

Opposite: Later medieval arms in the *Fenwick Roll* painted during the reign of King Henry VI, showing that, after nearly two hundred years, heraldic design had become more complex. The rule of colour never being placed on colour or metal on metal was frequently overlooked.
COLL. ARMS FENWICK ROLL 184-8

Depiction of a Tudor herald in an initial letter; William Dethick, Garter King of Arms from 1586 to 1604.
COLL. ARMS OLD GRANTS II P 90

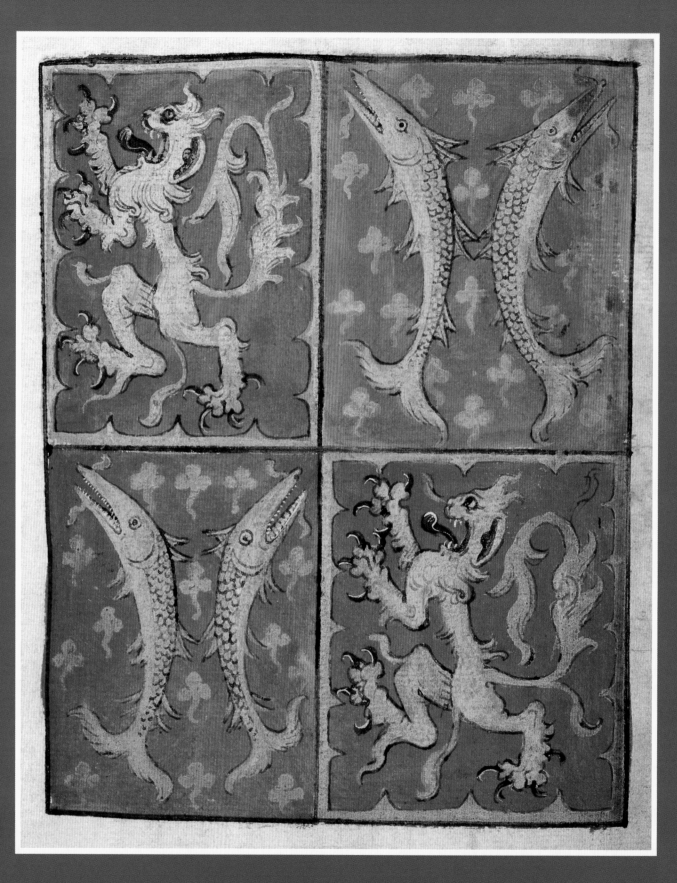

chapter 2

Fauna and Flora

Mammals, fish, birds, insects and plants

FROM THE BEGINNING heraldry's connection with natural history was apparent with the twelfth-century shield of Geoffrey Plantagenet, displaying its little lions of gold.

The lion holds an unrivalled position in heraldry. It has consistently been the most used of all heraldic charges, and has provided the heraldic painter with great scope for stylisation and varied interpretation. Zoologically, it was the only non-indigenous animal to feature significantly, or indeed at all, in early medieval heraldry.

Although the lion had once been native to Europe, by the twelfth century its presence there was confined to royal menageries. The menagerie maintained by Henry I at Woodstock housed a lion, and this possibly influenced the choice of the lion for Geoffrey Plantagenet's shield. This physical presence, together with the frequent mention of the lion in the Bible and classical

Opposite page: Stylised treatment of lions in the arms of Talbot painted circa 1450 and quartered with the luces or pike of Clermont.
COLL. ARMS TALBOT ROLL F 9

literature, combined with its traditional role as the king of beasts, was sufficient to allow it to surpass the native animals of Europe in its heraldic popularity.

One of the earliest extant rolls of arms is the thirteenth-century *Heralds' Roll*. An analysis of its 195 shields reveals that 43 feature a lion. Other animals appear on only ten other shields, a meagre number in comparison. Of these ten shields, one is charged with a bear, one with a crow or raven, three with luces or pike, three with eagles, one with a crane and one with a gryphon. Since the thirteenth century the lion's popularity has had its fluctuations; but its place as the pre-eminent zoological charge has never been challenged. Between l952 and l972 it featured in nearly 20 per cent of all supporters then granted. As such, its use has now surpassed that of the human being, which was far more widely used during the last century.

It is significant that the first two British monarchs known to have used heraldry were Richard Coeur de Lion of England and William the Lion of Scotland. Both had leonine nicknames and both bore lions on their shields. The first Great Seal of Richard Coeur de Lion is the earliest recorded example of the use of heraldry by an English sovereign. William de Barre states that Richard, when Count of Poitou, had been recognised through the lions grinning on his shield. This statement supports the view that Richard had adopted heraldry prior to his accession to the throne in 1189 and that the far side of his shield, hidden in his first Great Seal, featured a second lion. A later Great Seal struck in about 1195 introduced a third lion and arranged the animals in the manner used by all his successors. Unfortunately, this arrangement was to encounter an unforeseen difficulty.

During the thirteenth century, when heraldic rules and regulations had developed, together with the descriptive terms or blazons, it was held that the lion must ever be ramping on its hind legs with its face in profile. Another description was therefore needed for a lion walking on all fours with its head turned full-face, and the term 'leopard' was chosen. The expression 'the leopards of England' is one that tenaciously clings to life. However, by the beginning of the fifteenth century there was a growing preoccupation with the bestiary, which drew attention to this unfortunate nomenclature. The bestiary writers held that the leopard was

Eagles in arms, principally medieval, painted in the early sixteenth century.
Coll Arms L10 f 103b

31

Four crests demonstrating fanciful attributes found in the bestiaries:

Above left: The snake crest of Watson showing young snakes bursting from their mother's belly, granted 1580.

Above right: Beaver castrating itself, based on an entry for arms drawn in 1458, but apparently not granted.

borne of the adultery of a lioness with a pard, the latter almost certainly a cheetah. It was clearly not appropriate for the King of England to bear three bastards on his shields. Heralds therefore reverted to 'the lions of England', or more technically, 'lions passant guardant'.

With the exception of the lion, very few animals were used in early heraldry. Often these were intended to reflect characteristics admired by the user. The barons and knights of the Middle Ages were crude, rough men who mainly concerned themselves with war and self-advancement. When they were not preoccupied with pitting their strength against one another, they directed their attention towards the baiting and chasing of wildlife. Such basic and martial masculinity accounts for the use of stag, bull, bear, wolf and boar representing the pursued, with the greyhound, talbot (the heavier hunting hound) and birds of prey representing the pursuers. The martlet (which loosely covers the swift, swallow and species of martin) was symbolic of speed. So deeply engrained in the system did these characteristics become that even today many people would regard the foxhound as being more heraldic than the Pekinese or poodle; and the stag beetle to be preferred to the gentler butterfly. Political correctness should dictate that the Jersey

cow is as heraldic as the martial bull; but the acceptability of this may not be easy to achieve.

Only in the use of the pun did heraldry manage to flout the conventions of these animal characteristics with which medieval barons and knights identified. It accounts, for example, for a number of species of fish featuring in the arms of such families as Tench, Herring and Breme. Similarly the Lucys bore luces or pike, the Roches bore roach, the Ellises had their eels and the family of Gurney bore the somewhat unattractive but distinctive gournard.

It was not until the fifteenth century that heraldry turned its attention in earnest to the animal world and began recruiting the non-indigenous, a process that was stimulated by the practice of tournament participants adorning the helmet with a crest and their subsequent use of supporters. Here the medieval bestiary proved a rich source of inspiration. Two notable additions entering heraldry in this way were the elephant and the ostrich; the elephant (the Indian variety as opposed to its African relative) is frequently shown bearing a castle on its back that is clearly derived from the howdah. The ostrich may seem an unlikely bird to attract medieval attention, as today it is confined south of the Sahara. However, in

Above left: Hedgehog crest of Claxton showing roundels, presumed to be grapes, stuck on its spines, confirmed in 1561.

Above right: Crane crest of Petyt granted in 1690, typical of several where the crane is shown holding a stone. Although blazoned as a crane, it has been given a stork-like interpretation demonstrating the confusion which has long prevailed between these two ornithological families.
DRAWINGS BY GILLIAN BARLOW BASED ON COLL. ARMS MSS

the Middle Ages it had a much wider range and was well known in North Africa. The ostrich that entered heraldry held in its beak a key, horseshoe or other metal object, clearly an exaggerated reference to its liking for roughage to assist the gizzard.

Not indigenous to Britain but common in Europe, the pelican is usually depicted as an eagle-like bird vulning itself, that is to say, piercing its own breast and feeding the young with its own blood. Bestiary writers report that the male pelican killed his rebellious young and that it was the female bird which subsequently returned to the nest and restored them to life. There was hence an association with the resurrection of Christ; the pelican became a Christian symbol and is described in heraldry as being 'in her piety'.

Many of the bestiary animals with intriguing characteristics were ignored by medieval heraldry. The lynx, credited with remarkable eyesight capable of seeing through solid objects, did not acquire any popularity until the twentieth century; it is now an important charge in the heraldry of individuals or corporate bodies concerned with the eye. It would also make an appropriate charge for those involved with television.

It is intriguing to speculate what use might have been made of the curious characteristic attributed by bestiary writers to the castor, or European beaver. When pursued by its enemies, it castrated itself with its own teeth, being aware that the severed part of its anatomy was highly prized for medicinal purposes. Heraldry has yet to take and develop this idea, which must have potential for the imaginative herald.

More frequently, heraldry turned to the indigenous, adding to the small number of those mammals and birds found in the heraldry of earlier centuries, and embracing such humble species as the hedgehog, rabbit and squirrel. Once more, no attempt was made to check fanciful characteristics which were so often attributed to these creatures, and curious medieval accounts of nature passed unverified into heraldry. Heralds may have drawn on natural history; but they have never been natural historians. In consequence, heraldry shows baby adders bursting to life from their mother's belly and hedgehogs carrying falling grapes on their spines. The hedgehog was held to stand beneath trees of falling fruit; the fruit was impaled on its spines, thus enabling it to scurry

Indigenous birds in late medieval heraldry painted circa 1480.
COLL. OF ARMS M10 FF 74B/75

Left: The martlets of Sir John de Labere and the owls of Sir Thomas Burton.

Below: The herons of Sir William Heron.

off with a feast for its young. Cranes grasped stones in their raised claws to prevent them falling asleep. A crane dozing off would drop the stone on its foot and hence wake up; the stone-carrying crane is aptly described as a crane in its vigilance. The common crane was widely distributed throughout Western Europe and may even have bred in England. It was certainly much better known than the stork; and those who describe any indeterminate long-legged and long-beaked birds in heraldry as 'storks' should therefore be wary.

The use of zoology in heraldry reached a climax well before 1600. Later Tudor heralds never showed real inclination to move beyond the bestiary or native European species. Their predecessors had seemingly furnished them with enough material to create new heraldry without the need to look for fresh sources. Meanwhile zoological knowledge was increasing as travellers and explorers pushed back the frontiers of

Tragopan crest of Laward, alias Lord, of London, granted by Benolt and Wriothesley in the early sixteenth century.
COLL. ARMS L10 F 105B

the known world. Heraldry became introspective, taking no advantage of these new opportunities; and it was not until the nineteenth century that any attempt was made to catch up. Of the 182 grants of crests made by the kings of arms between 1674 and 1700, only seven feature non-indigenous animals: three cranes, which were by then extinct in this country, two peacocks, one camel and curiously one vulture – an uninspiring collection.

Any generalisation is bound to have exceptions; and sixteenth-century heraldic ornithology provides four interesting examples. The Chinese phoenix, based on the Argus pheasant, is discussed on page 79. Of the other three, the tragopan was granted as a crest to Robert Lord, alias Laward of London, by Sir Thomas Wriothesley, Garter King of Arms, and Thomas Benolt, Clarenceux King of Arms, in about 1510. Improbable though the bird may seem, it is not, as previously maintained, the product of Tudor imagination. The tragopan is a species of pheasant that displays horn-like wattles clearly exaggerated in the Lord grant. How or why a Himalayan bird came to be granted as a crest must remain a matter for further research.

In 1556 Thomas Hawley, Clarenceux King of Arms, granted the crest of a turkey to Robert Cooke of Mildham in Norfolk. The turkey's name is, of course, misleading. The turkey is a native of North America, and its introduction to Europe in the sixteenth century as a domestic fowl brought it to the attention of the heralds who used it, as a cooking bird, to provide a suitable pun on the grantee's surname. Presumably it was brought to Europe by the Spaniards and possibly made its way to Britain with Catherine of Aragon. The splendidly displayed turkey in Hawley's grant must therefore be one of the earlier depictions of the turkey in England, if not in Europe.

In 1591, Robert Cooke, Clarenceux King of Arms (not to be confused with the turkey grantee) introduced the bird of paradise as a crest for John Browne of Spexall in Suffolk. This bird was

Left: Thomas Hawley, Clarenceux King of Arms, granting the punning crest of a turkey to Robert Cooke of Mildham, Norfolk, 1556. The turkey reached Spain in about 1520 and England in the early 1540s.
COLL. ARMS GRANTS II P 453

Below: Bird of paradise crest of John Brown of Spexall, Suffolk, granted in 1591.
COLL. ARMS BEDN F 48B

doubtless that known by modern naturalists as the great bird of paradise. First knowledge of these birds was obtained through skins which were stripped of the carcase and legs. It was precisely this leglessness that gave rise to the belief of their continuous flight and hence their association with paradise. Cooke's grant is therefore accurate in depicting a legless bird.

The conservatism which manifested itself in the sixteenth century and prevailed throughout the seventeenth and eighteenth centuries greatly affected the use of zoological charges. The wolf remained popular, although the period saw its extinction in the wild. On the other hand, the far more common fox was generally considered as poor heraldic material except as a pun for such families as Todd. The fox had been regarded as vermin during the Middle Ages but there was to be a reassessment of its reputation with the development of foxhunting, a pastime enthusiastically adopted by a large proportion of Georgian and Victorian gentry. However, many of these were of recently acquired gentility, and in petitioning for arms they preferred the more traditional charges of heraldry such as the wolf, bear, falcon or stag, which reflected the field sports of the Middle Ages. They were thus trying to imply a medieval gentility, which would not have been suggested by the use of the newly appraised fox.

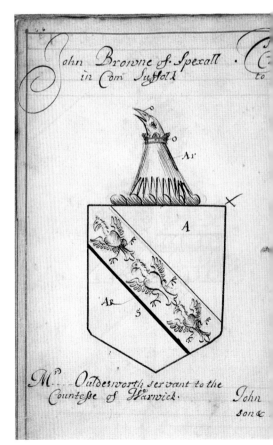

Top left: Ringtail possum crest of Jefferson, granted in 1982

Bottom left: Armadillo crest of Oliver, granted in 1989

Top right: Sloth crest of Baynes-Cope, granted in 1989

Bottom right: Agouti crest of Agutter, granted in 1996

Drawings by Gillian Barlow based on Coll. Arms MSS

Inroads into the conservatism of heraldry become apparent in the nineteenth century. Natural history, ever the provider of heraldic charges or devices, was central to this development and it remains at the heart of heraldry in the twentieth century. Take for example the 1,254 supporters granted by the kings of arms between 1950 and 1970. Of these grants, seventeen incorporate the kangaroo, compared with three between 1820 and 1920. Animals such as the zebra, giraffe, okapi and many species of antelope from the African continent, the bison, moose and beaver from North America, and the koala bear, echidna, and duck-billed platypus from Australia, have all made their impact on heraldic design.

Parrots in the arms and crest of Robert White of South Warnborough, granted 1513/14, are identified as Asian rose-ringed parakeets, the medieval 'popinjays'.

COLL. ARMS ORIGINAL GRANT

In addition, more obscure animals from Latin America like the armadillo, the coati, species of opossum, marmosets and even the sloth are no longer unknown in heraldry. One notable omission is the giant anteater. With its distinctive outline, and as an obvious pun for those named Anthony, it is surprising that, as yet, it has acquired no heraldic support.

While mammals were attracting new interest in the last century, species of non-indigenous birds were not so popular. Grants of supporters between 1820 and 1920 provided instances of new arrivals from the crane, stork and ibis group; beyond this only the emu, kiwi and tjarder were granted. However, since 1950 much wider use has been made of English birds, and non-European species have been recruited in increasing quantities. The weaver bird, kookaburra, penguin, secretary bird and the tui bird of New Zealand have been numerically the most conspicuous. Unfortunately, heralds displayed their ignorance of natural history in granting supporters to the Textile Institute of two weaver birds. Delightful though the birds may be, they are in fact red bishop birds, which are members of the false weaver bird family. Subsequent grantees associated with weaving or the Institute have requested this same bird; and an error has been perpetuated. It is to be hoped that future blazoning will be more specific, as the weaver birds cover many species of highly distinctive coloration, far removed from the red bishop.

The medieval popinjay is to be identified with the Asian rose-ringed parakeet. Today it has to share heraldry with other

The rhinoceros hornbill in the crest of Dickson, granted in 1997, has a distinctive outline well suited for heraldic design. It has featured in several crests in the late twentieth century.
PRIVATELY OWNED

members of the parrot family. In particular, species of Australian cockatoo have provided sound material for heraldic design, with their striking head feathers allowing for stylisation with simple and distinctive outlines. The cockatoo is merely one example of many species with these qualities which extend far beyond the parrots and embrace many ornithological families from every continent.

The twentieth-century spurt in ornithological interest may also be explained by the natural colouring of a bird's plumage, which is generally brighter and better suited to heraldry than the drabber, duller colours of the mammal. Once the lingering preference for depicting the mammal in its natural colours ceases to be an important factor in heraldic design, then perhaps it will match

Above: Africa, Australia and Asia are very well represented by the new species of birds entering twentieth-century heraldry. Species from Latin America, such as the resplendent quetzel, remain unusual. It features here in the crest of Hammond, granted in 1996. The Arms provide a pun with boars' heads for 'Ham' and a graded chief formation for 'mond(s)', which suggest Maya pyramids.
COLL. ARMS GRANTS CLXII p184

Left: Jackson's chameleon granted as supporters to Sir Clive Rose in 1994.
PRIVATELY OWNED

Frog crest granted to Edward Jackson in 1993. Frogs are also depicted in the decorated border of his letters patent and vair features in his arms.

the present popularity of the bird. There is, for example, no sound heraldic reason why an armadillo crest should be rendered in the animal's natural pinkish brown. Such treatment serves only to detract from the primary tinctures of the arms and introduce a discordant element into the overall aesthetic appeal of the design. Thankfully, recent armadillo crests have been rendered in gold or green with gold carapaces reflecting the tinctures in the arms and thus providing a greater unity of design. Examples such as this allow heraldry to remain an art form. Heraldry should not therefore be a field guide to the natural world, but should take species and evolve them to suit its own aesthetic aims and requirements.

With the exception of a number of snakes that feature in various knotted formations in late Tudor grants, reptiles are less popular as heraldic charges. Snakes are likely to retain a permanent position in heraldry as a component part in the rod of Aesculapius, the classical god of medicine, and in the caduceus or wand of Mercury, a charge suitable for those connected with the media or communication. The chameleon is a recent arrival, and its ability to change colour offers considerable scope for grantees involved with the theatre and even diplomacy. There are several species of chameleon which, with their various horns and facial embellishments, make for excellent and distinctive crests.

Until the late twentieth century, amphibians have never proved as popular as reptiles, with the notable exceptions of the frogs of King Pharamund and the sixteenth-century crest of Dryland, which shows a leaping frog as a delightful pun on the

Left: The punning stag-beetle crest of William Hartwell, granted circa 1501.
COLL. ARMS VINCENT 153 P 42

Below: Grasshopper crest of Sir Thomas Gresham, founder of the Royal Exchange, confirmed in 1568, the grasshopper or greshop being a pun on the surname.
COLL. ARMS G10 F 28

surname. However, the increasing interest in wildlife conservation and ecology may now boost the heraldic position of frog and toad. Since the natterjack toad attracted considerable national attention as 'Toad of Toad Hall' when it was granted as a crest for East Hampshire District Council, frog and toad have become increasingly popular. Whether sitting affronty or leaping in profile, they have artistic potential to compete with many of the stylised positions of the medieval heraldic lion. The newt, having digressed and evolved into the monstrous salamander, has also reappeared in late twentieth-century heraldry to start afresh as a natural animal, with its frilly dorsal crest allowing for a considerable measure of successful artistic licence.

The current interest in mammals, birds and to a lesser extent amphibians may soon be extended to fish and insects. The dolphin, regarded as the king of fishes in the Middle Ages, and the marine equivalent of the lion on land and the eagle in the air, was the only 'fish' regularly used in heraldry; other fish were generally restricted to the pun. However, game fishing has recently encouraged the use of salmon, trout and other more exotic species. The recent appearance of such varieties as sun fish, flying fish, parrot fish and angel fish reflect leisure interests in tropical climes, and on the periphery the fishing fly is proving an increasingly popular charge.

A limited number of insects, arachnids and crustaceans featured during the Renaissance and Tudor periods of heraldry; the grasshopper or greshop borne by Gresham and the stag beetle of Hartwell are two punning examples. More obscure is the sixteenth-century crest of Sharington, which features a scorpion. Perhaps the vicious stinging of the scorpion reflected a dry English humour and may also explain its reappearance in several twentieth-century grants of armorial bearings. Curiously the spider is largely absent, in spite of providing an obvious pun for the surname of Webb or Webber. In contrast the bee has had considerable popularity as a symbol of industry, and more recently the hexagonal cell formation of the honeycomb has been introduced several times as a field of the shield.

Recent invertebrate crests include the slater crest (below left) for Sclater, granted in 1988, and the water boatman crest (below right) for Hammond, granted in 1978.
DRAWINGS BY HENRIETTA WEBB BASED ON COLL. ARMS MSS

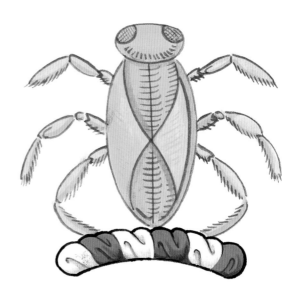

Twentieth-century heraldry has increased the range of invertebrates. The slater, a long and tiny derivative of the woodlouse, has been used as a punning crest for Sclater; and the water boatman displayed in gold is the crest for Hammond, alluding to the rowing interests of that grantee. Combining the pun and career is the elephant hawk moth granted as a crest to Lord Delfont. This insect provides not only a pun on Delfont but also an appropriate symbol for a patron of the theatre, as moths are associated with the bright lights at night. This is only one example of an increasing number of moth and butterfly armorials, which have also included larvae in the form of the silkworm caterpillar.

Elephant hawk moth in the armorial bearings of Lord Delfont granted in 1978. The moth provides a pun on his title as well as an allusion to his career as an impresario, moths being attracted to bright lights at night. Stars and flaunches feature in the arms with the latter suggesting theatre curtains.

<small>COLL. ARMS GRANTS CXLI P 199</small>

The mollusc has long been established as a heraldic charge. As a pun for families such as Shelley the choice of the escallop is obvious. More difficult to determine is to what extent its frequent appearance in heraldry derives from its adoption as a pilgrim's badge in the Middle Ages. In later centuries it acquired a maritime significance and proved an attractive charge for those grantees associated with the sea.

Whelks have provided a pun on surnames such as Wilkinson, while cowrie shells have featured in the arms of bankers (they were used as currency in various tropical cultures). There is also much scope for the mollusc in grantees concerned with building or engineering, or with any industry where there is an obvious emphasis on protection. Significantly the engineering company of Caparo has recently been granted four conch shells, which also allude to its connections with India where the conch is a symbol of the deity Vishnu. Other marine creatures such as a lobster and octopus have also featured in recent grants. These are creatures which are particular in having very distinctive outlines and provide excellent source material for heraldic design. The octopus, much favoured

Conch shells in the arms of Caparo Ltd, granted in 1997. PRIVATELY OWNED

in Greek and Roman art, is now known to have double vision and is equipped with a double brain system and a highly complex nervous system. Jacques Cousteau described the octopus as 'the soft intelligence'. The artistic potential of the octopus, when combined with these natural abilities, must surely place it among the more obvious devices to be used in future heraldic design.

Two varieties of animal fur have been widely used since the inception of heraldry in the twelfth century, reflecting sartorial

fashion of that period. Ermine is a white fur with black spots representing the tail of the natural animal, the stoat in its winter coat. Vair is composed of the grey-blue back skins of a species of squirrel found in eastern Europe, which are stitched alternately with the white belly skins. Originally both types of fur were probably stretched over the shield; but paint was subsequently substituted allowing either the ermine tails or the vair formation to be represented in different tinctures. A misunderstanding of the French word *'vair'* led to translators confusing this with *'verre'*, meaning glass. In consequence Cinderella was given impractical slippers of glass instead of fashionable squirrel skin.

Allied to these furs was a field known as papillonny, suggesting the scales of a butterfly's wing. Although rare in the Middle Ages, this type of field has recently sustained a revival and been used to suggest seats in a theatre or auditorium. Other allusions have included tiles on a roof and hence a suitable pun on such surnames as Tyler.

Zoological subjects have always featured far more prominently in heraldry than botanical ones. The rose, the fleur-de-lis, the garb or sheaf of wheat, and the simple devices of cinquefoil, quatrefoil and trefoil were alone in making any real impact on medieval heraldry. Trees, fruits and leaves made only rare appearances, usually as a punning allusion on a surname. Other forms of flora were negligible or nonexistent. Tudor heraldry attempted to rectify this, but in general its botanical charges played a secondary role to those of zoology. More often than not botany appeared in the

Lobster supporters granted to Baroness Wilcox in 1997. Her arms are depicted on a lozenge as appropriate for a lady peer.
PRIVATELY OWNED

Octopus badge of Chapman granted in 1995. The lozenges in the arms suggest sails reflected in white water as an allusion to sailing.
PRIVATELY OWNED

Roses in the arms, crest and badge of Cockshaw, granted in 1997.
<small>PRIVATELY OWNED</small>

form of a simple sprig held in the feet or mouth of a zoological charge to render this more distinctive from existing devices featuring the same animal. Too often the reason behind the choice of a particular plant remains obscure, but it is likely that the pun itself was a major factor.

The rose is exceptional. It is the botanical counterpart to the zoological lion. The plucking of red and white roses in the Temple Gardens by John Beaufort, Duke of Somerset, and Richard Plantagenet, Duke of York, is by tradition the origin of their adoption as badges of the rival houses of Lancaster and York. The truth is somewhat different. Henry III's queen, Eleanor of Provence, introduced a golden rose into English heraldry, and this was subsequently adopted as a badge by her eldest son, Edward I. Eleanor's second son, Edmund Crouchback, Earl of Lancaster, altered the tincture of his rose to red in order to distinguish it from that of his brother. Thereafter, the red rose adhered to the Earldom and subsequently Dukedom of Lancaster. Meanwhile the white rose had been adopted as a badge of the Mortimer family and as such is found in much heraldry of the Welsh Marches, the Mortimer stronghold. It was in consequence of his Mortimer descent that Richard Plantagenet, Duke of York, laid claim to the English throne and thus linked the white rose to the Yorkist cause. Some cinquefoils and even quatrefoils may also reflect the rose's influence on heraldry, being a simplified and stylised version of that flower. Others may derive from the pimpernel of Simon de Montfort and were a legacy of loyalty to his cause in the baronial wars of the thirteenth century.

The fleur-de-lis is one of the more controversial charges in heraldry. It is found in the arms of seemingly unconnected families throughout Western Europe, but it is most familiar in the royal arms of France. It passed into English royal heraldry when King Edward III laid claim to the throne of France and quartered the French fleur-de-lis with the English lions in 1337. It remained as a quartering in British royal heraldry until it was discarded in 1801. French tradition maintains that Clovis, King of the Franks, received the fleur-de-lis as a divine gift in return for his conversion to Christianity in 496. It is conceivable that Clovis, trapped between an army of heathen Goths and the River Rhine, noticed the water iris growing far out into the river. Recognising the possibility of fording at that point, he managed to lead his army to safety and subsequently adopted the iris, in the form of the fleur-de-lis, as his emblem.

Quatrefoils granted to Augustine Vincent, Rouge Croix Pursuivant, in 1621, being a variant of arms previously borne by his ancestors, which are depicted in the border.
COLL. ARMS ORIGINAL GRANT

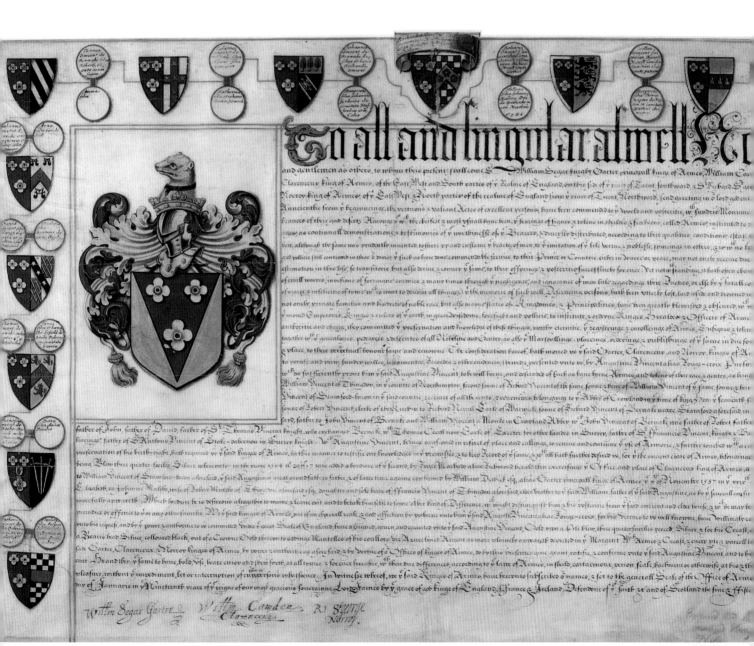

Fleurs-de-lis in the arms of Louis, Dauphin of France, later Louis XI, painted circa 1450. The dolphin in the arms and crest is a pun on his title of 'Dauphin'.

COLL. ARMS 1 M5 F 12B
(THE HYGHALMEN ROLL)

The first definite association of the fleur-de-lis with French royal heraldry dates from the reign of the twelfth-century king, Louis VII, hence the suggestion that the fleur-de-lis is a pun on the name Louis, the flower of Louis. There has been some speculation that the fleur-de-lis was a Moslem motif to which Louis was attracted while taking part in the Third Crusade. This seems unlikely as there is little evidence to suggest that, with the possible exception of mantling, Islamic culture had any influence on heraldry. Mantling, the stylised cloth draped over the helm and kept in position by a wreath, may owe something of its origin to the heat of the Mediterranean sun bearing down on the metal helmet. In spite of the participation of Louis VII in the Third Crusade and his adoption of the fleur-de-lis, the device has a pre-heraldic history and was previously associated with French royalty, featuring on crowns and sceptres. At the beginning of the eleventh century, Robert II decorated the rim of his crown with fleurs-de-lis and two hundred years earlier a fleur-de-lis formed the finial of Charlemagne's sceptre.

More intriguing are the arms which the Middle Ages subsequently attributed to King Pharamund, a black field charged with three gold frogs. King Pharamund was reputedly the great-grand-father of King Clovis, and he was said to have been descended from a river god. There is some indication that the Merovingian dynasty of France founded by Clovis paid special attention to the frog, giving it mystical qualities and using it as an emblem. This may account for those familiar fairy stories emanating from France, where frogs turned into princes and princes into frogs. It may also explain why the Flemings, during the Hundred Years' War, called their French neighbours by a nickname which was later revived by English sailors in the nineteenth century and translated as 'Froggy'. The golden water iris provides a habitat for the frog; and the one reflects the physical shape of the other. To what extent the link between iris and frog was recognised during the Middle Ages is a matter for speculation; but a frog origin for the fleur-de-lis must not be readily discounted.

The rivalry between England and France gave rise to the lion or leopard's face jessant de lis, which dates from the thirteenth century and shows the fleur-de-lis sprouting from the face of the lion, suggesting the English lion was gobbling up its French enemy. The combination, providing a single unified charge, had great potential; but the possibilities of this type of heraldry were not to be explored further until the twentieth century.

Before 1700 trees seldom feature in English heraldry. Of the nine thousand medieval shields collated in the sixteenth-century *Smith's Ordinary*, whole trees appear in only seven. Qualities of strength and endurance typified by the oak might have appealed; but somewhat surprisingly this did not happen. The tree was more often limited to a punning use until it had gained a new popularity in the eighteenth century, which was followed by a growing interest in flowers in the nineteenth. This heraldic use of botany can therefore be seen as reflecting contemporary gardening tastes, moving from the Georgian interest in landscape gardening to the herbaceous borders of the Victorians. In the twentieth century a wide range of flora has come into use, particularly from outside Europe. The dogwood of North America, hibiscus, lotus, the protea of South Africa and the Australian wattle and waratah flowers are examples that are now well established in heraldry.

Nonetheless, if the flower in pre-eighteenth-century heraldry was largely restricted to the rose, fleur-de-lis, the various foils and

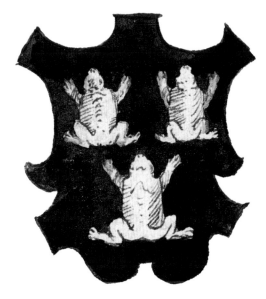

Three frogs in the attributed arms of King Pharamund, ancestor of the Merovingian kings of France. The frogs are sometimes denigrated to toads.
COLL. ARMS VINCENT 187 P 4

the secondary devices used in early Tudor heraldry, it had certainly established itself on the heraldic periphery. The flower was extensively used as decoration in the borders of letters patent issued by kings of arms when granting new armorial bearings. The practice of adding floral borders to these documents dates back to the fifteenth century when they were liberally sprinkled with the flowers of the countryside: campion, periwinkle, heartsease or wild pansy, honeysuckle, columbine and dog rose were most popular. It is significant that the heraldic principle of never placing gold or yellow on silver or white and vice versa was extended to these borders.

Daffodil, primrose and cowslip are therefore rarities. There seems to have been an inherent belief that yellow was lost against the white of the vellum background, demonstrating the heralds' preference for strong contrasting colours whether in heraldry itself or in this peripheral artwork.

One of the few native flowers to enter heraldry before the eighteenth century was the columbine or aquilegia. Its use was limited to a handful of armorial bearings, including those granted in 1461 to the Company of Cooks. Its inclusion here may result from a confusion with a type of ginger used for culinary purposes, and known as 'colambyne' as it was obtained from Colombo. Alternatively it may have been intended as a form of talisman or charm, for the columbine flower was held 'to be very medicinal for dissolving impostumations and swellings in the throat'. If this is so, then it represents a rare example of herbal lore in heraldry, two spheres of human activity which have otherwise remained far apart. What today is termed alternative medicine may have a heraldic future.

The rose is associated with England and its Scottish counterpart is the thistle. Unfortunately, the origin of Scotland's association with the thistle has been a victim of historical reassessment. The tradition that Scotland was saved by the thistle in 1263 has now been discounted. In that year it was held that the invasion of King Haco of Norway was finally defeated at Largs in Ayrshire by Alexander III, Haco's attempted surprise attack being thwarted by a cry of agony from one of his men who stepped barefoot upon a thistle. Apocryphal though this tradition may be, the thistle was adopted by James III, who used a thistle badge. This featured on his silver coinage of 1474.

LET EQUITY · PREVAIL

HONI SOIT QUI MAL Y PENSE

TO
Jones Esquir...
King of Arms Sendeth Gr...
NICHOLLS OF BIR...
Council hath represente...
Knight of the Most Noble...
Order Companion of the...
Excellent Order of th...
Decoration of the Milita...
that Her Majesty Th...
bearing date the Third do...
style and title of Baron...
of Surrey he is desirous o...
ity and hath requested th...
such Arms and Crest and...
be borne and used by hin...
And it being a privilege...
ship hath further requeste...
ing in the same Patent su...
as a Peer for Life the who...
as the said Earl Marshal...
Fourteenth day of Novembe...
and Crest and in the same...

LET · EQUITY · PREVAIL

Know Ye therefore that I the said Garter in pursuance of His Grace's Warrant a...
Me by The Queen's Most Ex- cellent Majesty do by these Presents grant and assign unto the s...
BIRKENHEAD the Arms following that is to say:- Sable two Bars each between two Cotises se...
Upon a Helm with a Wreath Or and Sable A demi Mole Sable holding between the paws a Daffodil slipped an...
ther grant and assign the following Device or Badge that is to say:- Within a Garland of Birch flowered Or a...
Daffodil slipped and leaved Or as are in the margin hereof more plainly depicted to be borne and used for ever...
head and by his descendants with their due and proper differences And by the Authority aforesaid I do further grant...
side a Cormorant wings displayed and inverted Sable beaked and legged Or as are also in the margin hereof more plain...
Baron Nicholls of Birkenhead as a Peer for Life and all according to the Laws of Arms In witness whereof I the said...
the Seal of My Office this Twelfth day of November in the Forty fifth year of the Reign of Our Sovereign Lady Elizabeth th...
Britain and Northern Ireland and of Her other Realms ...

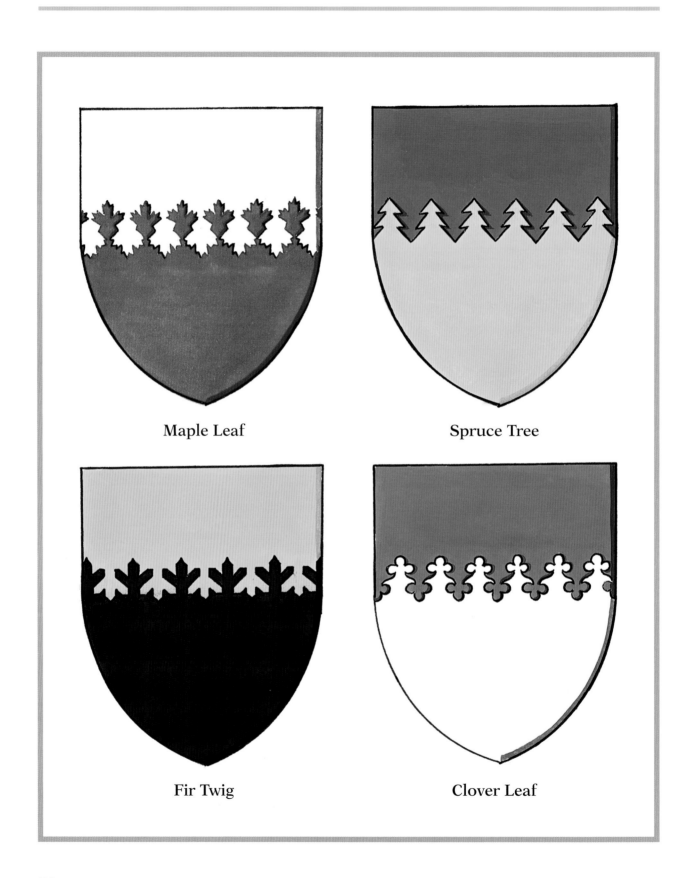

Maple Leaf

Spruce Tree

Fir Twig

Clover Leaf

A flower that has recently acquired considerable significance is the flax, associated with linen of Northern Ireland. Heraldry has been slow to recognise its importance, and the initiative has come from the Royal Mint, which has used the flax flower on coinage. Flax as an alternative to the Irish shamrock is now belatedly establishing itself as a familiar heraldic charge.

Leaves attracted little interest in the Middle Ages, but since 1700 their use in heraldry has been widespread. The spectacular rise in popularity of the maple leaf of Canada is possibly unsurpassed in modern times. In 1805 it is first mentioned as an emblem in the Quebec Gazette and soon afterwards it was incorporated as a device in the regimental colours of the Prince of Wales' Royal Canadian Regiment. Today it features in the royal arms of Canada, in the Canadian flag, and is frequently requested as a device by Canadians petitioning for a new grant of armorial bearings. In

Above: A leek in the crest of Howell granted in 1988.
PRIVATELY OWNED

Opposite page: Various division lines based on stylised leaves and flowers have been developed in Canada, Finland and South Africa. They may have a place in future English heraldry. Clockwise from top left, the lines are based on: maple leaf, spruce tree, fir twig, clover leaf.
DRAWINGS BY HENRIETTA WEBB

Mandrakes in the arms of Jennings granted in 1978. This knobbly forked root resembles the human figure and was thought to be the embodiment of some curious underground monster which commanded respect, not least because the mandrake was believed to have aphrodisiac properties.
COLL. ARMS GRANTS CXL P 309

1988 the Queen established a separate heraldic authority in Canada; and this authority has since devised intriguing divisions of the shield where the dividing line terminates in a series of maple-leaf outlines. This stylisation of the leaf or flower to provide new partition lines has also been successfully developed by the South African heralds with the protea flower; it is a type of design which may well have artistic merit and deserves to be explored further.

Fruits are largely confined to punning use, with a few exceptions. One such is the pomegranate, where its numerous seeds make allusion to the seeds of learning. Similarly the hazelnut provides a welcome relief from the over-used open book and torch of youth for places of education. The hazelnut and its tree have pre-Christian connotations, as the hazel is the pre-Christian tree of wisdom. Likewise, the mistletoe, with its pre-Christian attributes as an all-heal and a symbol of life, is a fitting charge for medicine and health. Heraldry has now caught up with the mistletoe and recognised its significance, which in the meantime had lingered on over the centuries and survived into the twentieth century with Christmas kissing. This is a remarkable achievement for a plant with no known edible or medicinal qualities.

Vegetables have been largely ignored by heraldry with the exception of the Welsh leek and a limited interest in the mysterious mandrake. The mandrake's root was thought to resemble the human figure and when hauled from the ground issued a shriek causing madness to those who heard it. Less tiresome was the leek. The Tudor livery colours of green and white have an ancient Welsh history. There is a contemporary reference to Llewelyn the Great clad in royal robes of green and white silk. Later Edward, the Black Prince, ordered cloth of 'green and white' to make short parti-coloured coats and hats for his Welsh troops. They were thus the first to appear on a continental battlefield in national uniform.

Although no medieval source describes the leek as a Welsh emblem, its wearing was an established custom in Tudor times. The natural green and white of the vegetable suggested the royal robes of the ancient princes; and this is probably no coincidence. The twentieth-century intrusion of the more aesthetically pleasing daffodil may have upset Welsh purists, but it must not be forgotten that the daffodil was also known as St David's leek.

Above: In twentieth-century heraldry, the fleur-de-lis has been further combined with the animal in the design of badges.
Top: Knowles, granted 1975
Centre: Baxter-Wright, granted 1984
Bottom: Zawoda-Martin, granted 1992
DRAWINGS BY GILLIAN BARLOW BASED ON COLL. ARMS MSS

Left: A precursor of a number of twentieth-century badge designs, the arms of Morley, painted in 1661. Zoology and botany were combined imaginatively in the thirteenth century with the lion or leopard's face jessant de lis, possibly indicative of the English lion swallowing the French lily.
COLL. ARMS M7 P 60

chapter 3

Heraldic
Monsters

Dragons, gryphons, unicorns, tygers and other monsters

POPULAR BELIEF TENDS to credit heraldry, and hence the heralds, with the invention of such fabulous beasts as the gryphon, unicorn and cockatrice. Flattering as this may be to the heralds, it is incorrect.

It fails to take into account the medieval bestiary, one of the few widely read books in the Middle Ages. The medieval bestiary was based on the work of Physiologus who, at some unknown date between the second and fifth centuries AD, wrote his book of beasts, on to which was grafted the factual and fanciful writings of many later authors. The medieval bestiary made no attempt to differentiate between these facts and fancies, and its readers happily accepted that a gryphon or unicorn was as real as the animals that surrounded them in daily life.

Although the occasional monster found its way into early heraldry, it was not until the fifteenth century and the need to provide for animal supporters that the bestiary became a major source for heraldic design. Subsequently new crest material was required

These be the Armes of Antyquite of the
wourshipfull company and felowship of the

when the Tudor heralds accepted that crests were appropriate for all those persons or families already bearing arms or those newly created as armigerous gentlemen. Hitherto crests had been in limited use, and the majority of shields of arms had been borne without them.

Probably the first of the bestiary monsters to feature in heraldry was the gryphon. In 1167 it appears on the seal of Richard de Redvers, Earl of Essex. Medieval bestiaries state that the gryphon had the size and strength of over one hundred eagles and possessed the ability to seize and carry off an ox in each claw. It was also the guardian of mines of gold which were hidden in high mountains where the gryphon built its nest lined with the same precious metal. There are accounts of feuding between gryphons and a race of horse-borne Scythians who attempted to steal the gold. In consequence bitter antipathy arose between gryphons and horses; and it is tempting to think that this bestiary account encouraged knights to charge their shield with the gryphon in an impractical attempt to instil fear into the horses of the opposing cavalry. Goblets believed to be fashioned from gryphons' claws or eggs were highly prized in the courts of medieval Europe. These were almost certainly made from antelope horns and ostrich eggs.

The association of gold with the gryphon can be traced back to Aristeas, a remarkable Greek traveller of the seventh century BC. Aristeas journeyed to the mountains of central Asia and returned to report of a people who stole gold from fearsome creatures which he called gryphons. This points towards the lammergeyer or bearded vulture which is a huge bird with a wing span of nearly 10 feet. The lammergeyer nests in inaccessible cliffs in the Asiatic mountains and is reputed to seize and carry off live sheep. The gold of lammergeyer territory is real enough and continues to be mined today. The association of the gryphon with gold ensures its place in twentieth-century heraldry as an appropriate charge for individuals or corporate bodies associated with finance.

Aristeas would seem to have been responsible for reinvigorating a tradition found in his native Greek culture. His account of the gryphon was grafted on to an existing gryphon which, judging from seal depictions, had a Middle Eastern origin. This earlier gryphon may have been nothing more than a composite creature, the symbolic combination of the eagle, the king of the birds, and

Dragon in its two-legged form,
known as the 'wyvern',
supporting a banner of the arms
of the Principality of Wales,
painted mid-sixteenth century.
COLL. ARMS VINCENT 152 P 96

the lion, the king of the beasts. Such symbolism is understandable;
but the trail to the earlier nature of the pre-Artistean gryphon then
diversifies and becomes obscure. At one extreme, there is ancient
Egyptian mythology with its emphasis on composite creatures, and
at the other the intriguing suggestion that the gryphon may have
originated from dinosaur remains. The *Protoceratops* of central

Cockatrice supporting the arms of Sir William Kingston, Knight of the Garter, who died in 1540. COLL. ARMS VINCENT 152 P 107

Asia was once abundant. It was a four-legged creature, albeit wingless, with a beak and an armoured frill to its face which could account for the stylised ears of the gryphon. However, this theory bypasses the Middle East unless the migrations of people are taken into account. Such migrations took place but they were so distant in time that a straightforward composition of the much-respected lion and eagle seems more likely than any lingering memory of a central Asian fossil.

The dragon was another creature that arrived early in heraldry. Currently it is much favoured by Welsh grantees and also by those associated with the City of London; two dragons feature as the supporters in the City's armorial bearings. Like the gryphon, the dragon has remained largely unaltered by centuries of heraldry, except for an extra pair of legs which it gained in the fifteenth century, for which the heralds seem largely responsible. The earlier dragon with its two legs is now termed a 'wyvern', and the later four-legged form remains the dragon.

As with the gryphon, a dinosaur origin has been suggested for the dragon. It is argued by some that an Indo-European tribe may have discovered the fossilised remains of *Tyrannosaurus rex* or some other prehistoric carnivore. As complete dinosaur remains lying exposed are virtually unknown, this theory must be treated with scepticism.

The dragon now associated with heraldry certainly has a pre-heraldic history. It was brought to Britain by the Romans who are said to have used it as a badge for their cohorts. The Romans were seemingly inspired by Dacian tribesmen whom they conquered during the reign of the emperor Trajan at the beginning of the second century. The Dacians, who occupied territory immediately north of the Danube, used long windsock banners, in the mouths of which they placed lighted tapers or torches.

These banners were called 'dracones', and may have been responsible for the wings of the dragon of heraldry and also for its traditional fire-breathing qualities. Dacian windsock banners were merged with the dragon of the classical bestiaries where the dragon is described as the largest of the snakes and which lassoed its prey in a knot with its tail, leading to suffocation. It is not difficult to see the python in this description. The Roman affiliation with their dragon was retained by the Romano-Britons, where the Welsh word *draig*, or dragon, was synonymous with 'leader', and the attributed arms of Uther Pendragon were two green dragons with gold crowns charged on a gold field.

If the winged python of the West is accepted as a basic dragon form, it must not be confused with the dragons of the Orient. Chinese dragons, for example, are wingless and bewhiskered monsters, closely associated with water and having the interesting ability to change size. The watery element indicates a crocodilian origin. This delightfully evolved monster is a welcome latecomer to heraldry and is now chiefly found in the armorial bearings granted to persons or corporate bodies which have Far Eastern affiliations.

Another snake, the cobra, has also played a part

Unicorn as a supporter to the arms of George Augustus Frederick, Prince of Wales, later King George IV, painted in 1803. COLL. ARMS BATH BOOK

HIS ROYAL HIGHNESS
GEORGE-AUGUSTUS-FREDERICK
PRINCE OF WALES.

in the creation of fearsome heraldic beasts. Both cockatrice and basilisk have cobra ancestry. Although the basilisk is now depicted in heraldry with the additional dragon's head at the end of its tail, the cockatrice and basilisk are otherwise the same. The creature was never the size of a dragon; the bestiary writers give it no more than 6 inches in length. Nonetheless, it was regarded as the king of all snakes; the name basilisk derives from *basileus*, the Greek word for 'king'. The venom of basilisk or cockatrice was so deadly that even birds flying above it were overwhelmed and would drop dead from the sky. Nonetheless it had an enemy; it could be overcome by 'weasels'. Although weasels do not prey on snakes, the mongoose does. Accurate medieval natural historians simply did not exist and the idea of weasel and mongoose being interchangeable is more than acceptable. The medieval suggestion that a cockatrice could be overcome by a mongoose points to the cobra, a snake considerably smaller but more deadly than the python. The coxcomb of the cockatrice is explained by the inflated hood of the cobra. Once the head of the creature had been associated with a cock, further fancification took place. The cobra was turned into a deadly monster half-cock and half-snake, and reptilian rather than feathered wings were added. Further factors were introduced by Alexander Neckham, a so-called naturalist whose imaginative writings were to prove influential in determining much fanciful medieval thought on natural history. In about 1180 Neckham stated, without any apparent foundation, that the cockatrice was hatched from the egg of an aged cock incubated by a toad; later versions credit the snake with being the incubator. So great was the subsequent fear instilled by this finally evolved cockatrice that in the fifteenth century a cock was put on trial in Basle charged with laying an egg. It is not known how the trial went except that the cock was found guilty in spite of having its own defence counsel. It is to be wondered how the cock and his counsel managed to communicate.

Although popular in more recent centuries, the unicorn was a rarity in medieval heraldry. Bestiary writers likened Christ to the unicorn, and its use in heraldry was therefore regarded as blasphemous. The fabulous and miraculous horn of the unicorn was considered to be the most valuable of all charms against poison and sickness; and that belonging to Queen Elizabeth I was valued at

Opposite page: Harpy crest of Sir John Astley, who died in 1486. The harpy, described by Virgil as 'of Monsters all most monstrous this', never obtained the heraldic popularity of other fearsome monsters found in the bestiary such as the dragon, gryphon and cockatrice. 'Political correctness', with its emphasis on equality for the sexes, suggests that the harpy may be the monster that tried but failed to establish an influential position in heraldry.
THE KNIGHTS OF THE ORDER OF THE GARTER, ST JOHN HOPE, LXIX

Opposite page: Yale supporter of Henry Carey, created Baron Hunsdon by his cousin, Queen Elizabeth I, in 1559.
COLL. ARMS VINCENT 152 P 108

£100,000. This and other such horns can now be identified as the spiral horn of the narwhal, a species of small whale found in the northern seas which sports a tusk of fine ivory that can reach the length of 7 or 8 feet.

There are two generally held theories on the unicorn's origin. First, it is believed by some that it originates with the Arabian oryx, a species of desert antelope. The second theory favours the single-horned Indian rhino. Both theories are unsatisfactory. Neither takes into account the medieval legend of the unicorn, which described its mode of capture: a virgin, preferably naked, would be sent into the forest, whereupon the unicorn would then come and lay its head trustingly in her lap and follow her faithfully wherever she went. This legend, together with the horn, an obvious phallic symbol, has strong pagan and sexual undertones. Similarly, oryx and rhino do not provide an explanation for the well-known nursery rhyme: 'The lion and the unicorn were fighting for the Crown; the lion beat the unicorn all around the town.' The enmity between the two is found in much early mythology. Frequently the lion chases the unicorn across the sky and slays it. The lion is known to have been a solar symbol; and the sun, in turn, was sacred to the ancient gods of the Indo-European peoples. By inference the unicorn was a lunar symbol, and this is borne out by its frequent appearance on ancient seals and coins where it is shown in conjunction with the crescent moon. The moon was associated with the goddesses of the Indo-Europeans, who were largely governed by matriarchal systems until they were replaced by male-dominated societies several thousand years before Christ. The unicorn's goddesses linger on in the guise of the medieval virgin of the unicorn legend. This legend was adapted by Christianity, the virgin being identified with the Virgin Mary and the unicorn with Christ.

The unicorn may well have had a composite origin, being constructed from parts of several distinct animals each sacred to a particular season of the year, with the horn as a fertility symbol. It is significant that Ctesias, in about 400 BC, states that the unicorn's horn was white, red and black, colours that represent the stages of womanhood. White represents the virgin, red is for the sexually active woman and black for the aged hag. If the unicorn was not a calendar creature, it may have had a natural origin. Many of the

ancient goddesses are known to
have been associated with the white
bull. It is conceivable that one or
more matriarchal tribes was able to
graft the horn buds of a young
white calf on to the centre of its
forehead. This is physically possible
and intriguingly results in a single
massive horn.

The gryphon, dragon, cockatrice and unicorn were familiar
monsters of the bestiaries and as
such remained largely unaltered by
subsequent heraldic use. However,
less familiar creatures underwent a
process of heraldic evolution. With
the adoption of three-dimensional
crests in the fourteenth century and
the appearance of supporters in the
fifteenth century, there was a need
for new source material. Supporters
in particular required beasts with
claws and feet, to enable them to
support shields of arms. Clearly
geometrical or inanimate objects
could not fulfil this need; and
accordingly the heralds turned to
the bestiaries as well as to the natural world around them. During the
sixteenth century the heralds
became bolder and more imaginative; and by the end of the Tudor
period some remarkable changes
had taken place. Animals that had a
natural origin were fancified and
developed into creatures far
removed from this origin and can
therefore be regarded as heraldic
monsters in their own right.

The Honorable Henry Brooke
Lorde and Baron Cobham

SCIRE SAPERE FACERE

Opposite page: Heraldic
antelope and dragon as
supporters in the armorial
bearings of Henry Brooke,
Baron Cobham, painted in 1616.
COLL. ARMS E16, F 42B

Left: Heraldic tyger in the arms
and crest of Thomas Sybell,
confirmed in 1531.
COLL. ARMS D13 F 2

The male gryphon crest for Wickham-Smith, granted in 1974.
COLL. ARMS GRANTS CXXXVI p 237

One of the new arrivals, dating from the beginning of the fifteenth century, was the yale. This is first found as a supporter in the arms of John, Duke of Bedford, who adopted it as a punning allusion to his Earldom of Kendal or Kend-eale. Bestiary writers report that the yale had the remarkable characteristic of being able to swivel its horns at will, laying one back in battle and keeping it in reserve in case the forward attacking horn sustained damage. The yale is also reported to have enjoyed wallowing in water. Medieval mapmakers frequently scattered drawings of animals over their land masses. In these drawings the yale is consistently depicted as an animal of the East. This does not suggest the African wildebeest which has often been favoured as the origin of the yale. Its appearance in the East and its liking for water point instead to the water buffalo. This creature attacks with sudden swipes of the horn, which perhaps accounts for the swivelling characteristics found with the yale.

Although comparatively slight, the evolution of the yale in heraldry can be found in the treatment of its horns and tail during the course of the fifteenth century. The early Bedford yale had straight horns and a long tail. It subsequently passed with the earldom to Sir John Beaufort, Duke of Somerset, and thence to the latter's daughter Margaret, Countess of Richmond, mother of Henry VII. By the end of the fifteenth century, this Beaufort yale had evolved into a creature with convoluted horns and a short tail. As such it featured as one of the Queen's beasts chosen from past Royal Heraldry to stand in sculptured form at the entrance of Westminster Abbey at the Coronation of Queen Elizabeth II in 1953.

A more noticeable evolution is found with the heraldic antelope. Reported in the bestiaries as essentially a gentle animal, it can be identified with the blackbuck, which was then widely distributed in the Middle East before it retreated to its present limited range in India. Heraldic evolution changed the blackbuck into a creature of ferocious countenance with tushes, a tusked nose, and sprouting tufts of hair. It also acquired serrated horns which were doubtless an exaggerated and stylised representation of the spirals found in the horns of the actual animal.

The heraldic tyger proved particularly popular in the heraldry of the early sixteenth century. This too had been found in the bestiary where it was correctly placed between lion and leopard. Bestiary writers drew attention to its qualities of ferocity and speed. It was native to Persia; the Persians called their arrows *tygris* and named their principal river the Tigris.

Readers of the bestiary were also advised to be wary of travelling in tiger territory and to carry with them one or more looking-glasses or mirrors. Guillim advises that, on being charged by a tiger, the traveller should 'use a policy to detainne their damme [the female tiger with cubs] from following them by casting sundry looking-glasses in the way, whereat she useth to long to gaze, whether it be to behold her own beauty or, because she seeth one of her young ones and so they [travellers in Persia] escape the swiftness of her pursuit.' Strangely, the bestiaries do not report the tiger's stripes, but Persian tigers are known to have had less pro-

Opposite page: Male gryphon as
the sinister supporter to the
arms of St Leger, confirmed in
1531, showing horns and hairy
mane.
COLL. ARMS G2 F 24

nounced stripes than tigers today. The tiger or tyger came into heraldry as a cat-like creature, albeit unstriped. It was accompanied
by its looking-glass but this was soon discarded as an awkward
encumbrance. Heraldic evolution then enhanced its ferocity by
providing it with a wolf-like face, adding serrated ears and adorning the creature with a horn or tusk on the end of its nose. This
heraldic tyger in its fully evolved form is essentially a creation of
heraldry and bears little resemblance either to the natural animal
or to the original tiger of the bestiaries.

Even more extreme than the heraldic tyger is the case of the
male gryphon. This creature is easily confused with the more
familiar gryphon with its eagle wings. The male gryphon has a
wingless body which is notable for its emission of sparks of fire.
Why this creature became known as the male gryphon remains a
mystery; but this nomenclature does not imply that the winged
animal was female. Heraldic depictions of the winged creature
have invariably provided it with a suitably masculine anatomy.

A clue to the origin of the male gryphon is to be found in the
supporter to the arms of St Leger painted in 1530. This shows a
creature with a hairy mane, two horns, and sparks of fire emanating from wither and rump. Here is a creature midway in the
process of heraldic evolution. Ultimately, feathers replaced its
hairy mane and the horns disappeared. It seems likely that these
changes were not deliberate but rather the result of misinterpreta-
tion. A bad rendering of a hairy mane could easily be mistaken for
feathers leading to an error which was adopted by later heralds
and herald painters as a model for new designs. This is doubtless
the explanation of much heraldic evolution, which was essentially
haphazard rather than deliberate.

The male gryphon of St Leger provides vital clues as to the
origin of the creature. Its hairy mane and two horns can be linked
to bestiary writings. The only creature in the bestiaries to be possessed of mane and horns is the bonacon. The bestiaries also recite
that the bonacon defended itself by means of a fiery emission from
its backside which was capable of setting fire to everything con-
tained in several acres behind it. The likelihood is that the heralds
and their painters found bestiary descriptions of the bonacon that
did not specify the part of the anatomy from which the fire came.
Fiery emissions were therefore placed at random on the creature's

Opposite page, top: Panther supporter to the arms of Jane Seymour, third wife of Henry VIII, painted circa 1536.
Coll. Arms M7 p 17

Opposite page, bottom: Various stages of the evolution of the heathcock or moorcock from the natural blackcock.
Drawings by Henrietta Webb

Styrian panther in the arms and crest of Styria, painted in the fifteenth century.
Coll. Arms B23 f 29b

body. One such emission may have come from the mouth and was subsequently mistaken for a beak.

With the bonacon, identification with a natural animal becomes possible. Some bestiary accounts state that the bonacon's horns curled back on themselves so that if you collided with the animal you did yourself no harm. It is also reported that the creature was reddish in colour and had a woolly mane. All this points directly to the European bison, *Bison bonasus*.

Although the male gryphon is confined to English heraldry, a similar process of evolution took place on the continent, where the steer evolved into a creature known somewhat improbably as a panther. The Styrian panther with eagle claws is also depicted with sparks of fire emanating from beak and backside. A steer as a pun on Styria is likely to be its origin. Clearly the rumbling bowel movements of the bovine family made an impression on the bestiary writers.

The early Tudor period witnessed the high point of the heraldic evolution of monsters. There then appears a growing awareness that misinterpretations had taken place. In some instances there was even a reversion to the original bestiary form.

This strengthens the argument that the evolution of monsters was largely the result of mistakes and not part of any deliberate process. An example of such reversion is to be found with the salamander. The salamander had evolved into a fire-breathing dog-like monster with a lion's tail as exemplified in the Garter stallplate of Sir James Douglas, Earl of Douglas and Avondale circa 1461 (see page 91). It was subsequently to revert to something nearer its origin as an amphibian which in turn approximates to its description in the bestiaries. Salamanders whether of canine or amphibious nature were always held to be so cold that they sought refuge in the hottest flames where they survived unharmed. This fanciful characteristic has allowed the salamander, wrapped in its flames, to be a popular charge in the heraldry for such as fire authorities. There is, of course, no good reason to associate the natural salamander with fire. That the bestiary accounts were accepted for so long was largely due to that highly respected Renaissance artist and

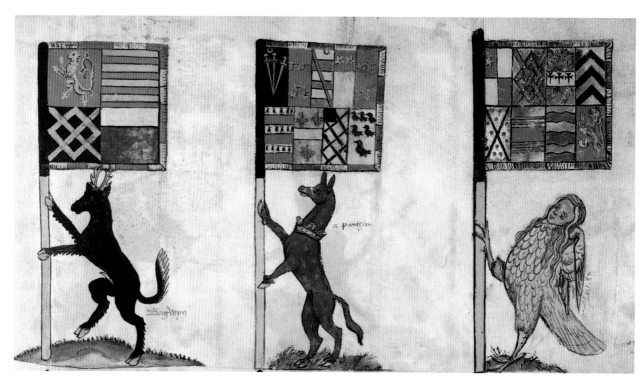

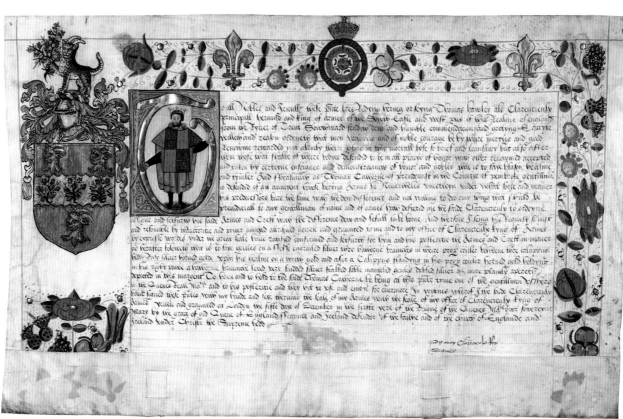

silversmith, Benvenuto Cellini, who recalled that in 1505 his father saw in the midst of the hottest flames a little animal like a lizard which was sporting about in midst of the most scorching blaze. Few were prepared to question such a reputable source of information.

A further example of the reversion of the process of heraldic evolution is found with the supporter of Jane Seymour, the third wife of Henry VIII. Although this supporter is a panther, it is depicted with multicoloured stripes. It seems likely that the creature was based on a bestiary where colours were mentioned, but no indication was given as to how these colours were arranged. The resulting evolution proved unacceptable; and later members of the Seymour family reverted to the more familiar spotted panther.

Although the panther lost its stripes, it sustained another change which proved to be more permanent. Sir William Segar, Garter King of Arms, writing at the beginning of the seventeenth century, states that 'this beast... is admired of all other beasts for the beauty of his skyn being spotted of variable colours; and beloved and followed of them for the sweetness of his breath that streameth forth of his nostrils and ears like smoke, wch our paynters mistaking corruptly do make fire.' In this form it is known as the 'panther incensed'; and it is significant that 'incensed' can mean either enraged or sweetly smelling. The kindly disposed panther of the bestiary was thus transformed by herald painters into a monster characterised by fire, flames and ferocity. Segar's observation once more emphasises that heraldic evolution was largely a process of chance and error. The original panther or pard of the bestiaries is likely to have been a cheetah. The leopard was thought to have been the bastard offspring of a lion and the pard. The natural leopard is more akin to the lion in shape; but it has a spotted coat similar to the longer-legged cheetah. In this way the leopard has inherited some characteristics from both of its supposed parents.

Above: Alphyn crest granted to Hicks in 1997.
PRIVATELY OWNED

Opposite page, top: (from left to right) Bagwyn, pantheon and harpy painted in the sixteenth century. Whereas bagwyn and pantheon appear to have been the product of Tudor imagination, the harpy has a long history in medieval and classical bestiaries.
COLL. ARMS VINCENT 152 P 98

Opposite page, bottom: Calopus crest granted as a pun by Thomas Hawley, Clarenceux King of Arms, to Thomas Cathorne of Pembrokeshire in 1553. As its name suggests, it is an amalgamation of cat and antelope.
COLL. ARMS ORIGINAL GRANT

The evolution of heraldic monsters was not confined to the mammal. Birds were also subjected to similar treatment. A good example of such evolution is to be found with the heathcock or moorcock. A study of contemporary renderings of the bird during the Tudor period shows how it originated with the blackcock, which was then abundant in southern England and the midland counties before its retreat to the north. Initially the bird was treated to an exaggeration of its wattles so that they came to resemble the comb and wattles of a domestic cockerel. Thereafter came the elongation of the tail feathers. At first this elongation retained the distinctive lyre-like formation found with the natural bird; but ultimately the tail feathers were straightened and swept upwards into two sharp points resulting in a creature far removed from its natural origin. The heathcock or moorcock is still usually shown with black plumage in heraldry, which thus provides a tenuous link with the blackcock. In time this particular link may be severed, and the bird rendered in the full range of heraldic tinctures.

In addition to drawing upon the bestiaries, early Tudor heralds made use of their own fertile imaginations to create new monsters. Among these creations were a number of composite creatures such as the comparatively simple bagwyn, essentially a roebuck with a wolf's tail, through such as calopus and calygreyhound to the more complicated enfield with the head of a fox, the chest of a greyhound, the talons of an eagle, the body of a lion and the hind legs and tail of a wolf. One such creature which is currently enjoying a revival in popularity is the alphyn; a popularity based largely on the pun. This composite creature combines the body of the heraldic tyger with the forelegs of an eagle. It is also characterised by a knot in its tail for which no explanation has ever been offered.

Arguably more aesthetically successful than these composite monsters is the pantheon. Unknown to the bestiary writers, the pantheon would seem to be the product of early Tudor imagination which held that the creature inhabited the starry skies. It was thus normally depicted in purple or black and liberally sprinkled with estoiles (stars). Currently it too is enjoying an increase in popularity in an age where scientific technology is frequently involved with space.

A whole group of composite Tudor monsters relates to a belief that all creatures on land had their counterparts in the sea. This idea was sometimes extended to counterparts in the air. Tudor heralds made good use of this idea and duly placed wings, scales, fins and fishtails on a variety of land creatures. This practice has been revived in recent years; and modern grants of arms frequently include marine or airborne monsters. Some combine all three elements so that, for example, the crest of the Brisbane Chamber of Commerce is a winged sea bull.

Although they drew heavily upon the bestiaries and their own imagination, Tudor heralds showed a surprising reluctance to utilise the new discoveries made by contemporary explorers and travellers, a reluctance which continued well into the nineteenth century. An exception to this was the Chinese phoenix, granted to two City livery companies in the fifteenth century. This reflects the City of London's interest in foreign trade and a growing awareness of the Orient's importance. The Argus pheasant is native to China and in Chinese culture had evolved into the *feng huang*. As such, it was found by Western travellers who confused it with the classical phoenix of the bestiary. Once transferred to Europe, the *feng huang* sustained further alterations and evolved into what is now termed the Chinese phoenix. The classical European phoenix of the bestiary had a different origin. It was derived from a real eagle which

Above: Crest of a Chinese phoenix of Briggs granted in 1967. This exotic fowl is derived from the *feng huang* of China, based, in turn, on the Argus pheasant. It differs from the classical phoenix, which originated with the eagle. Grants CXXX p 184A

Opposite page, top: Seacalf crest granted to Thomas Metcalfe in 1555 is not only a pun but also manifests the frequent addition of marine characteristics to land-borne animals much favoured by Tudor heralds. Tudor marine monsters were covered all over with fishy scales; later heralds usually followed the mermaid precedent by simply adding a fish's belly and tail to a mammal or bird. Coll. Arms MS G10 f 59

Opposite page, bottom: Winged seabull of the State Chamber of Commerce and Industry (Queensland) granted in 1991, following in the long tradition of making land animals additionally marine or airborne. Coll. Arms Grants CLVI p 334

Catoblepas crest of Ward
granted in 1984.
COLL. ARMS GRANTS CXLIX P 239

with painted wings was burnt alive with spices in a nest of palm branches by the ancient Egyptians. This took place at Heliopolis every 160 years as a sacrifice to the sun and the celebration of the leap year.

The failure of Tudor heralds to adopt the new discoveries of the sixteenth century marks the beginning of a conservative age in heraldry. From the late sixteenth century for some 250 years, heraldry was to remain essentially retrospective, preferring to rearrange old and by then well-established creatures rather than branching out to seek new additions to its monstrous menagerie. The heralds turned instead to the human being as an inspiration for crest and supporter material. There follow serried ranks of supporters consisting of naval and military figures and natives of conquered territories. These clearly reflect Britain's preoccupation with its developing empire. Similarly, crests frequently made use of the human arm with the hand grasping numerous different objects.

This conservative period in heraldry lasted until well into the nineteenth century before there occurred a reawakened interest in monsters which has survived and flourished to play an important part in the heraldry of today. The medieval bestiaries have again proved a rewarding source of material. Two recent additions to heraldry transported from the bestiaries are the caladrius and the catoblepas. Bestiary writers stated that the caladrius was a bird that drew sickness out of an invalid with its stare. It would then fly up towards the sun where heat consumed the disease; and in this way the invalid was restored to health. Although the bird of the bestiaries has the appearance of a gannet, it may well have evolved from the calandra lark, which has a high, soaring flight, thus explaining the bird's association with the sun.

The catoblepas was located in Africa and had a characteristic heavy head which bent downwards towards the earth. Other bestiary writers likened the catoblepas to a bull. These descriptions indicate the wildebeest; but later writers fancified it beyond recognition. The monster described by Edward Topsell, writing in 1607, was a beast all set over with scales like a dragon. It had no hair except on its head, great teeth like swine and had wings to fly and hands to handle. In this form, it has found its way into twentieth-century heraldry.

There are likely to be many successors to the caladrius and catoblepas. At this time of writing, grants of armorial bearings are being prepared that incorporate the hierocosphinx (a winged lion with leonine head replaced by that of a falcon) and a horse-headed eagle. In addition the cultures of other countries are providing source material. This is particularly true of the cultures of the Orient and the Native Americans, where centuries of evolution have, as with the *feng huang*, resulted in characteristic monsters which are now proving an asset to current heraldic design.

Chinthe supporters granted to Sir Nicholas Fenn in 1997, an example of fanciful creatures coming from the Orient, in this instance, Burma.
PRIVATELY OWNED

chapter 4

The Art of
Heraldry

Origins; changing styles; choice of devices

Opposite page: Simple
geometric forms of bars, bends
and crosses in early medieval
heraldry probably originated
with bands of metal
strengthening the wooden shield
and providing added protection;
painted circa 1365-70.
COLL. ARMS MOWBRAY'S ROLL F 10

IN THE DECORATION of the twelfth-century Renaissance shield,
it seems likely that much use was made of the existing structure of
wood, metal and leather. A high proportion of early heraldry consisted of bands in horizontal, vertical, diagonal or cross formation
painted in contrasting tinctures.

Much has been written to attribute qualities to each of these
tinctures, reflecting an erroneous assumption that most medieval
armorial bearings had specific meaning. In England this can be
traced back to John de Bado Aureo writing his heraldic treatise
Tractatus de Armis in the last years of the fourteenth century. De
Bado Aureo and subsequent writers provide a variety of different
qualities for each tincture. Gold, for example, shifts from being the
tincture exclusively used by royalty to that associated with obedi-
ence. Faith was another attribute of gold and as such it must have
overlapped with blue as the tincture of loyalty. Blue also varied as
a tincture of war and of peace and friendship. There is nothing to
indicate that medieval heraldry incorporated these ideas or that

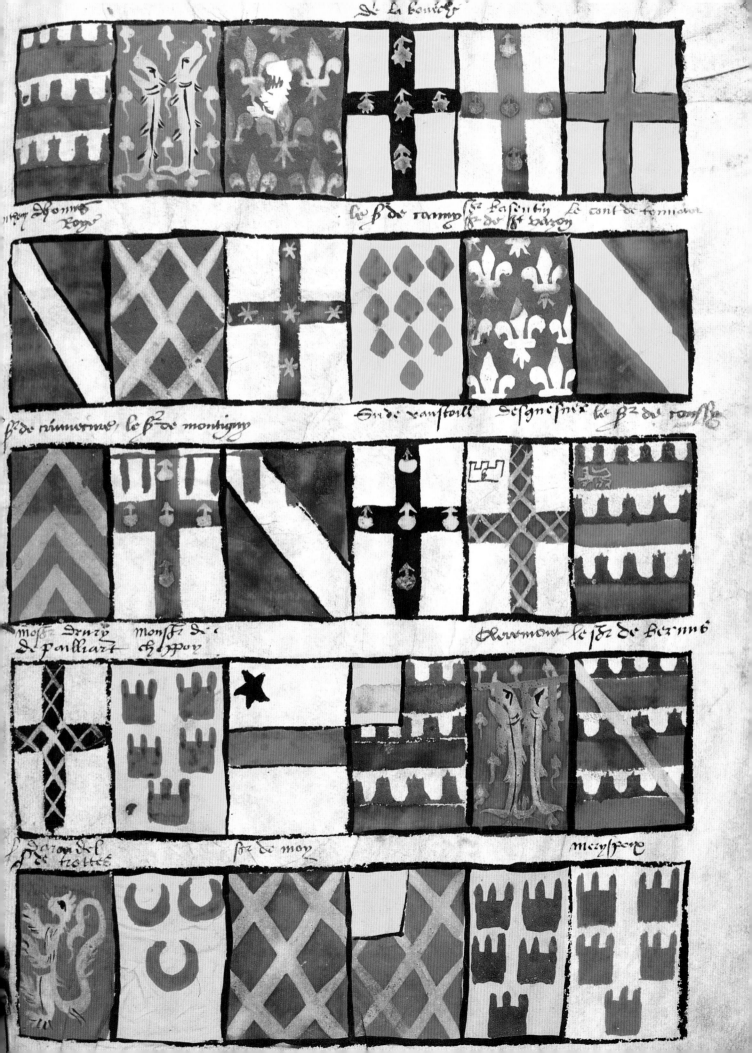

Cross formations which may
have evolved from a central
boss.

COLL. ARMS HOLLES' ORDINARY P 239

they have in any way affected post-medieval heralds in their task of designing new armorial bearings. Joseph Edmondson in his *Complete Body of Heraldry*, written in 1780, puts the matter in perspective: 'but as to such ridiculous fancies, the mere mention of them is fully sufficient'.

In addition to strengthening and protective bands of metal, there were studs and bosses which, when painted in different tinctures, would give rise to distinctive forms and may account for the use of many roundels or circles in early heraldry. Similarly the central boss mentioned by Anna Comnena may have developed into the escarbuncle, a boss-like formation with decorated spokes. Later theories attribute the cross to the presence of the original user of the arms on a crusade. However, a shield strengthened with one vertical and one horizontal band would provide a cross formation, and a decoratively treated stud or boss could account for the use of a variety of smaller crosses as individual heraldic charges.

The incidence of simple charges in early heraldry is demonstrated by the crescent. *Smith's Ordinary*, compiled in the sixteenth century, contains nine thousand medieval arms. Of these, 168 are listed under crescents; nearly one in fifty shields therefore bore this charge. It seems doubtful that medieval knights were inspired to adopt an Islamic device, as is often claimed by their descendants, who overlook the fact that none of their ancestors took part in a crusade. It is possible that cognate heraldry played its part, that is to say the adoption of the crescent from the existing arms of a family connected by blood or feudal tenure. However, the frequent use of the crescent suggests that it had a more practical origin. The addition of a simple sliver of metal to a shield would serve to deflect opposing weaponry; practicality in the twelfth century may have meant that the crescent was no more than a glancing device used to ward off a sword or an arrow at an oblique angle.

The evidence that pieces of metal were used as deflecting devices on shields is given further credence by the mullet which has a five-pointed star formation and is frequently pierced in the centre. The term 'mullet' means 'little mill', referring to the spur rowel. As a small sharp piece of metal, it may have been hammered on to the shield for protective purposes and subsequently painted in heraldic tinctures. Two hundred and eighty shields charged with mullets are found in *Smith's Ordinary*. If mullets and

Opposite page: Crescents may have originated with pieces of metal hammered on to the shield to act as weapon deflectors; painted circa 1380.
COLL. ARMS JENYNS' ORDINARY F 25

Below: Mullets are frequently shown pierced, indicating their origin as a metal spur rowel. Rings or annulets are also likely to have been metallic. Both mullets and annulets may have been originally used for protective reasons and are here shown in the arms of De La More; painted circa 1480.
COLL. ARMS M10 F 152

crescents were used in this way, it is possible that such charges as annulets or rings and billets or rectangles may also have originated as pieces of metal employed as protective devices. Smith lists ninety-three shields with annulets and seventy-three with billets.

In decorating the existing structure of his shield, the medieval knight was inspired by that love of ornamentation characteristic of the twelfth-century Renaissance. Although tinctures were seldom, if ever, chosen for symbolic reasons, the preference for strong contrasts was responsible for the principle that colour (sable, azure, gules and vert) was never placed on colour, nor metal (argent and gold/or) on metal. The limited use of vert in early shields of arms is explained by the fact that it did not stand out against the natural colouring of the countryside.

In addition to allowing the structure of the shield to dictate the nature of much early heraldry, the medieval knight drew heavily upon fauna, exercising a subjective desire to be associated with the masculine and warlike characteristics of certain animal species of which the lion was pre-eminent. Many also wished to demonstrate a blood or feudal link with other families. Groups of similar arms borne by connected families therefore developed and are known as cognate heraldry.

Sir Anthony Wagner, Garter King of Arms from 1961 to 1978, demonstrated the importance of the swan in early cognate heraldry and in doing so showed that pre-heraldic legends may have provided the inspiration for the choice of certain heraldic charges. One such legend, dating from the eleventh century, tells how an unknown knight disembarked from a river boat towed by a white swan in order to protect the widowed Duchess of Bouillon and her daughter Beatrice. The knight subsequently married Beatrice and imposed on her an oath never to question him as to his birth. A daughter, Ida, was born to the couple before Beatrice asked the fatal question. The swan knight departed as he had come and was never heard of again. Ida later married Eustace, Count of Boulogne, and many of their descendants adopted the swan as their heraldic device. Other versions

of this same legend suggest that the swan knight rescued and married the widowed Duchess of Brabant; and their descendants also adopted the swan in their heraldry.

The cognate is also apparent in the heraldry of the Washington family. In 1182 William de Hertburn acquired the manor of Wessyngton in the County of Durham and in consequence he and his descendants took the surname of Washington. It is thought that the original William was the son of Patrick of Dunbar, the second son of Earl Gospatric of Dunbar. Certainly thirteenth-century members of the Washington family bore a lion on their shield similar to the lion of the Dunbars. In 1278 Robert de Washington held the manor of Routhworth from the Barony of Kendal. The Barons of Kendal bore *Argent two Bars Gules*; and Robert de Washington exchanged his lion for the well-known arms, *Argent two Bars Gules in chief three Mullets also Gules*. Entitlement to these bars and stars was ultimately vested in George Washington and may be responsible for the familiar Stars and Stripes of the American flag.

A charge that is constantly used in medieval heraldry is the cinquefoil. Its use combines the cognate with the pun. Puns have a long history in heraldry and are the reason for the choice of numerous charges. Some cinquefoils are now believed to have originated with the pimpernel flower adopted as a punning device by Robert FitzPernell, Earl of Leicester. The earldom and the pimpernel flower, stylised into the cinquefoil, subsequently passed to Simon de Montfort, Earl of Leicester, in the thirteenth century. In the baronial wars which split England during the reign of Henry III it seems likely that many of de Montfort's supporters incorporated the cinquefoil in their arms, to demonstrate their allegiance.

The combination of punning and cognate heraldry explains much of the popularity of the martlet (i.e. the swift, swallow or martin) in early heraldry. Although the speedy flight of the martlet may have had an attraction in its own right, families such as Valence and Arundel chose it as a pun. *Volans* means 'flying' and *hirondelle* is the French for 'swallow'. Both these powerful families had ramified connections with other families who thus chose the martlet to feature in their arms, once again to show allegiance.

The pun also explains the use of many inanimate charges which might otherwise have had limited or no appeal. Leaky is said to have borne water bougets or goatskin containers; Seffington bore scythes and Shakerley and Shuttleworth bore shuttles. Spades were adopted by families of Standelf, Gardner and Swettenham; a delf is that which is delved or dug, and vigorous digging usually produces sweat. Other inanimate charges such as bugle horns and horseshoes were frequent in medieval heraldry; horseshoes were borne by families of Ferrers, Ferounes, and Shoyswell; and horns by families of Horne, Horner, Forrester and hence Foster and Forster.

Over the centuries romantic tales have often arisen to account for the choice of charges in medieval heraldry. Most of these tales are little more than flights of later imagination, and there is no evidence to support them. For example, the Prince of Wales's badge of feathers was long held to have been adopted by Edward the Black Prince from the crest of the blind King of Bohemia, who was slain at the Battle of Crécy in 1346. This story ignores the fact that the crest of King John consisted of two eagles' wings scattered with linden leaves. It also overlooks the use of

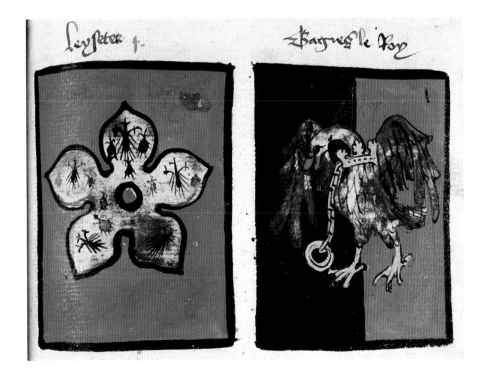

The swan badge of Bohun, inherited by Henry V through his mother, Mary Bohun, adjacent to the Leicester cinquefoil; painted circa 1480.
Coll. Arms MS M10 f 129

ostrich feathers by some of the Black Prince's brothers. It is now
recognised that the feathers were introduced into English royal
heraldry by Philippa of Hainault, the mother of the Black Prince.
The feathers are thought to have originated as a punning allusion
to Ostrevans, a continental county held by her family.

Sceptics tempted to dismiss fanciful tales should be wary.
There are a few medieval heraldic charges which could indeed owe
their origin to unusual events. For example, in 1330 Sir James
Douglas undertook to convey the heart of Robert Bruce to
Jerusalem for burial. Sir James was killed on the journey and the
heart of Bruce was brought back to Scotland. Thereafter a heart
was incorporated in the arms of the Douglas family.

Another tradition which may have substance surrounds the
FitzGerald monkey. The tale is told of Thomas FitzMoric, the thirteenth-century forebear of the FitzGeralds, Earls of Desmond. On
the news of his father's death 'Suddainly the nurses running forth
cryeing and lamenting the childe was left all alone when a monkey
that was kept in the house tooke him out of the cradle, carried him
to the topp of the castle, there unwrapped him out of swaddling
clothes, licked and lapped the childe and folded ye childe up in
cloathes againe and... brought him downe againe in safety and left
the sayed child where he found him, and finding the nurse settled
by the cradle gave her a sound boxe on the eares, as it is thought
thereby warneing and admonishing her to looke better hereafter
to her charge.' The crest of the Earls of Desmond is a boar; but
another branch of the family, the Earls of Kildare, bears a monkey.
This suggests that it may have been John FitzThomas FitzGerald,
first Earl of Kildare, an exact contemporary of Thomas FitzMoric,
who was carried off by the monkey. According to this legend, the
infant was rescued by the castle monkey during a fire.

There is a story about a twelfth-century Welsh chieftain by
the name of Moreiddig Warwyn which also may have substance.
Warwyn means 'fair neck' and may refer to a birthmark. Medieval
superstition attributed this to an adder which frightened his mother while she was resting in the garden during her pregnancy. The
mark of the snake was laid upon the neck of the child, his place of
birth was named Lle-Dychrynllyd, the place of horror; and his
descendants thereafter bore a boy's head with a snake entwined
about the neck.

mon̄ · ſtͤōnamys · dovglas

mon̄ꝰ · iamis · le · coūtͤ · de · dovglas

The Fitzgerald monkey in the arms of William Robert Fitzgerald, Earl of Kildare, painted in 1774.
COLL. ARMS PEERS I P 66

Other tales involving children include the eagle fostering an early ancestor of the Stanleys, Earls of Derby, in its nest; and it is to be wondered what lies behind the remarkable crest of Saunderson with a wolf's head either gorging or disgorging a baby.

As the Middle Ages moved towards their close, several developments in heraldic design become apparent. Early heraldry had shown a reluctance to place one charge upon another. Invariably a plain fess or a chevron had been placed between three other devices of similar nature. Gradually it was accepted that these devices could be placed on the fess or chevron, thus making it possible to add three further charges to the shield. This greater complexity of the arms was to be exploited by the early Tudor heralds, and led to a style of heraldic design far removed from anything known to their medieval predecessors.

A second development in the late Middle Ages comes from the granting of arms to corporate bodies such as the mercantile companies of London, beginning with the grant to the Drapers Company in 1438. Such grants frequently incorporated charges which reflected the craft or trade of the grantee. In consequence a number of inanimate objects unknown to early heraldry were introduced; occupational heraldry had come into existence.

With the incorporation of the royal heralds in 1484 and the subsequent increase in Tudor bureaucracy, a more efficient system of record-keeping emerged. It therefore becomes gradually easier to identify the original grantee or bearer of the arms and to learn more about him. In consequence this sometimes helps to shed

The Stanley eagle and child crest painted circa 1470. A fourteenth-century Latham ancestor of the Stanleys is stated to have adopted an infant which an eagle brought to her nest. The child was made heir of Latham and became the father of Isobel Stanley. Variations on this legend are given, but all suggest that illegitimacy may have been involved.

COLL. ARMS M3 F 34B

Above: Crest of Saunderson of Lincolnshire based on a drawing circa 1590.
DRAWING BY HENRIETTA WEBB
BASED ON COLL. ARMS VINCENT 182 P 111

Opposite page: Bulls' heads, lozenges, anchors and garbs charged on bends in the *Fenwick Roll*, temp. King Henry VI. This charging of the basic geometric forms of heraldry was a late medieval development.
COLL. ARMS FENWICK ROLL 149-152

light on why particular charges were selected. At the same time the granting king of arms becomes known and his personal preferences in terms of design can be discerned.

At the time of the incorporation of the royal heralds, John Writhe was Garter King of Arms, a position which he held from 1478 to 1504. Grants of new armorial bearings made by John Writhe and his fellow kings of arms during the two-year reign of Richard III numbered five, namely Whiting, Rede, Gough, Horton and the Company of the Wax Chandlers. Of the personal grants only Rede included a crest, that of a duck, possibly a shoveller. His arms also bore three similar ducks. The use of the duck, with its association with reeds, is clearly a pun on the surname, proving that the pun was still a current source of inspiration. Of the remaining personal grants, Horton is notable for including *a Fess compony counter compony between three Crossbows*. The reason behind the crossbows may be elusive but they are probably an example of occupational heraldry. In contrast the compony fess in checkers of blue and murrey demonstrates allegiance to the House of York, these being the Yorkist livery colours. Inclusion of royal livery colours is a feature of several fifteenth-century grants of arms and extends also to the blue and white of the House of Lancaster. Cognate heraldry, in common with punning heraldry, had therefore survived the Middle Ages.

The limited number of grants of armorial bearings known to have been made by John Writhe and his fellow kings of arms at the end of the fifteenth century is misleading. This was a period enormously rich in heraldic creation. Hitherto unknown badges and supporters were numerous, but the documentary letters patent issued by the kings of arms granting these devices seem nonexistent. The power to grant and confirm all armorial bearings had been vested in the kings of arms since the early fifteenth century, but this may have been interpreted as applying only to the shield of

Caryngton. Cobham.

Waller. Maundre. Caryngton. Boteler. Cosby.

Dudley. Otteley. Godyngton. Naufant.

fiz mary. Hanton. Foy. Wylbode.

Thomas Seymer de londoñ

Willm Belhowse de Rebatt Surrey

John Caryll de Warnehm de Suffex

John Hartshane Lincolñ

Willm boughton esquier de corps de littil lalleford Warwikshire

Richard Bateby de Cokehm barkshire

Robert Barowe de Flokerbroke en la comtee de Chestre

James Spenser

arms itself. Badges and supporters were therefore considered not to come under royal jurisdiction and letters patent conferring them upon grantees would not have been thought appropriate. Another possible reason for the lack of documentary evidence for the granting of badges and supporters is that it was only the upper levels of arms-bearing society who possessed these heraldic accessories, persons whose gentility was never in doubt and who therefore required no letters patent to prove or establish their social status. On the other hand the style of heraldic design during this period suggests a common designing source, presumably the heralds. This is particularly the case with the monster supporters of the late fifteenth century, where such as pantheon, bagwyn and enfield appear to come from the imagination of one man or from a group of men.

It seems likely that the kings of arms were therefore far more active in designing new heraldry than the surviving documents would imply, only issuing letters patent to those whose right to bear arms might be challenged. Discussion and informal sketches rather than formal documentation may have been considered sufficient. This may explain the absence of any documentation for the grant of the College of Arms itself; for no one would dispute the right of the kings of arms to grant armorial bearings to their own corporation. Curiously what they actually granted to themselves remains in doubt. Early sixteenth-century sources blazon and depict the four birds set around a central cross as falcons. Later they became accepted as doves, an allusion to the medieval heralds acting as messengers.

Writhe's son, Sir Thomas Wriothesley, succeeded his father as Garter King of Arms in 1505 and held that office until 1534. Wriothesley and his contemporary, Thomas Benolt, Clarenceux King of Arms from 1511 to 1534, were responsible for a period of heraldry uniquely creative and distinctive. Approximately five hundred armorial bearings granted by Wriothesley and Benolt have been identified. With the exception of those to women and clergymen, all include a crest. This was a major break with medieval practice where the crest was seemingly limited to those of tournament rank. Wriothesley and Benolt allowed crests to be granted with all arms, while still restricting the use of supporters; and this practice still persists today.

Opposite page: The early sixteenth-century heraldry of Sir Thomas Wriothesley showing heavy charging of the arms with different devices. Crests are frequently charged with bars, bends or chevronels.
Coll. Arms MS L10 f 108b

John
x. Northall

Meezy
heathh

fr Richard
Sutton

Rauf
Dodmer
de london

Thomas
somer
salop

Wiltm
de london

marshall
psr me
poth

Richard palsted suffolk
p me Johem
huske

Richard
off bishop

fishaz
hatfeld
heath

george Poll de
stebe stone de wyf

Opposite page: Characteristic of Wriothesley heraldry was the widespread use of flora with the principal device in the crest frequently holding or placed between sprigs of foliage.
COLL. ARMS L10 FOLIO 93

Left: The Garter stall plate of Sir Richard Beauchamp, Earl of Warwick, who died in 1439, showing the feathers of the swan crest continuing into the mantling. Such mantlings, characteristic of the Middle Ages, had been replaced by mantlings of red lined with white by the end of the fifteenth century.
THE KNIGHTS OF THE ORDER OF THE GARTER, ST JOHN HOPE, XXXIV

A typical Wriothesley/Benolt crest was treated to many of the divisions previously found only in the shields of arms of medieval heraldry. Whereas a medieval crest was usually rendered in a single tincture, a Wriothesley/Benolt crest frequently consisted of an animal divided by paly, barry, quarterly or bendy formations. Flowers and sprigs of foliage were then set on either side of the

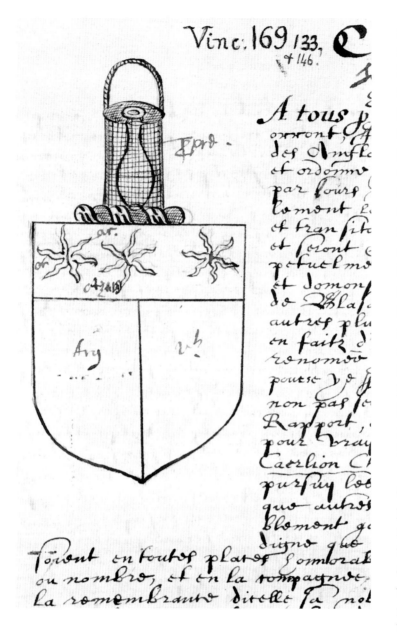

Vinc. 169/133,
(+ 146?)

'Ung orynall dedens son case en leurs propre coleurs', a urinal in its basket, granted as crest by John Writhe, Garter King of Arms, to Louis Caerlion in 1493.
COLL. ARMS GRANTS VII P 401

animal or placed in its beak, mouth, foot or claw. The shield itself drew heavily upon the late fifteenth-century practice of charging the basic geometric forms, or ordinaries, with a further device. Arms typical of the period contain two or three charges combined, for example, with a chevron or fess. Further complexity was often achieved by the addition of a chief or broad horizontal band at the top of the shield, upon which further charges were placed. This early sixteenth-century heraldry is in stark contrast to the simplicity of medieval heraldry. Some purists may argue that it is cluttered and lacking in control, but it is nonetheless exciting and allowed English heraldry to break away from its medieval restrictions, thus providing for future freedom of design.

The proliferation of complex crests during this period was accompanied by a simplification of mantling. During the Middle Ages this stylised cloth or mantle placed over the helm had been treated in a variety of tinctures and forms. Some mantlings were sprinkled with badges and others were an extension of the crest and so composed of fur or feathers. By the end of the Middle Ages mantling was largely standardised in the national tinctures of red and white, as found with the red cross of St George set on its white field. The vast majority of mantlings remained in these tinctures until the mid-seventeenth century, when there was a sudden shift to the use of the principal colour and principal metal taken from the arms. This later development can be seen as a distinct improvement, since it created a better unity of design.

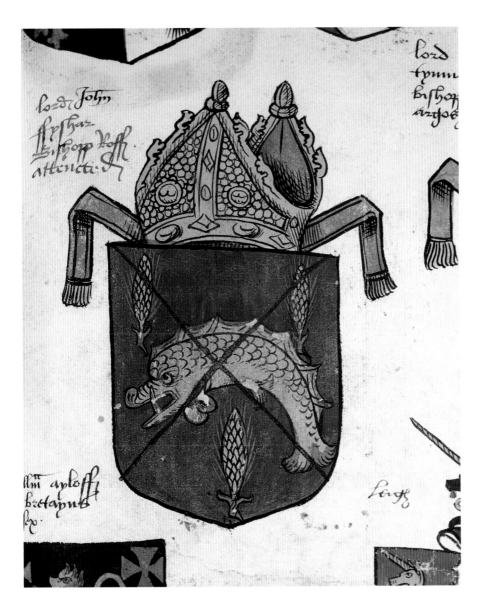

Above: Typical puns of the early Tudor period (from left to right):

Richard Chopping:
a woodpecker, the ornithological chopper, granted circa 1532.

Ralph Warren:
a rabbit standing within a warren, granted in 1528.

John Pasmere:
a sea hare ('puss' is a term used for a hare, and *mare* is Latin for sea), granted in 1520.

George Robinson:
robin and sun, granted in 1528.
DRAWINGS BY HENRIETTA WEBB
BASED ON COLL. ARMS MSS

Left: The defaced arms of John Fisher, Bishop of Rochester, beheaded in 1535, incorporate a dolphin traditionally regarded as the king of fishes and three ears of wheat, thus the pun 'fish-er' (ear)
COLL. ARMS VINCENT 153 P 227

Right: Grant of arms by Thomas Hawley, Clarenceux King of Arms, in 1549 to William Stompes of Malmesbury. Hawley introduced a simpler form of design. He greatly favoured engrailing, here used in the per chevron engrailed division. Combining this with three animals or animal heads is another Hawley characteristic.

COLL. ARMS ORIGINAL GRANT

Opposite page: Grants of armorial bearings made by William Hervey, Clarenceux King of Arms, circa 1558, including a master cook to the Queen and the Lord Mayor of London and his wife, whose arms are shown without a crest. Wriothesley's influence on Hervey's heraldry was greater than that of Hawley; it therefore looked back to the early sixteenth century rather than forward to Cooke and subsequent seventeenth-century kings of arms.

COLL. ARMS L9 F 25

Unfortunately, the reason behind Wriothesley's choice of charges is too often obscure. Cognate heraldry accounts for the frequent and continued use of blue and murrey, the earlier Yorkist livery colours, as well as the more familiar green and white of the Tudors. Association with the crown may also account for the many Wriothesley grants incorporating the greyhound, a creature much favoured by the Tudors, Henry VII using two greyhounds as his supporters. Occupational heraldry is not immediately obvious. Although John Writhe in 1493 had granted to Louis Caerlion, doctor of medicine, the now celebrated crest of a urinal in a basket, during the Wriothesley/Benolt period such an obvious allusion to the grantee's occupation seems to have been confined to simple charges, for example bezants or gold roundels for a goldsmith. In contrast there was liberal use of the pun. Many are obscure and it seems likely that the great majority have still to be identified.

Lowxe
of Cornewaill

George webster
my cooke to
the quenes matestie

Sir John wright
mayor of London

Katherin Boden
widdow difford
wright

Edward wilkinson
my cooke

John Bulberte
of knygeston

William fforde
goldsmyth
of London

Robert Payne
goldsmyth of
London

Typical grants made by Robert Cooke, Clarenceux King of Arms 1567-93 (with one by his successor, Richard Lee), showing a simpler style of heraldry than that prevailing at the beginning of the century.

COLL. ARMS PHILLIPPS MS 11223 P 121

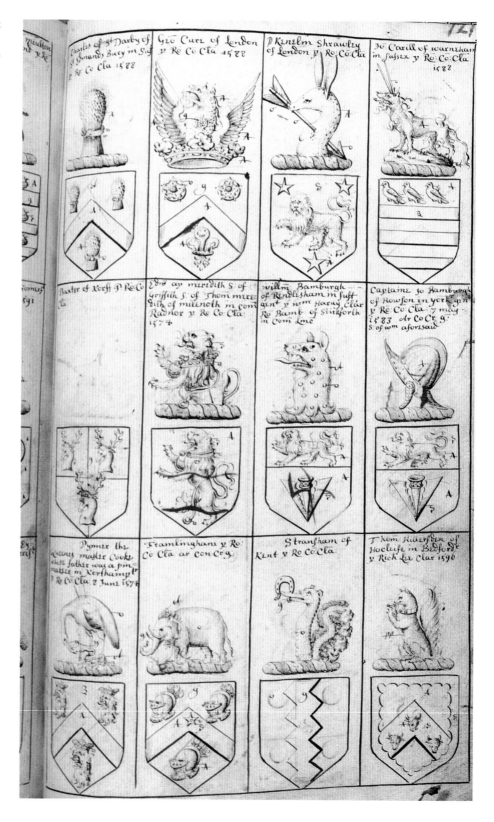

In the mid-sixteenth century heraldic design returned to simplicity. This was largely due to Thomas Hawley, Clarenceux King of Arms from 1536 to 1557. In the design of arms Hawley favoured engrailed crosses or chevrons, placing these between animals or animal heads. No further charges were added. His crests lacked the geometric patterning of the Wriothesley/Benolt period. Pages of similar Hawley grants demonstrate that the personal tastes and even whims of individual heralds have played a major part in heraldic design and the choice of charges. At times these would seem to have dominated to the near exclusion of any wishes or preferences of the grantee. This is not necessarily a flaw in the system. The herald is the expert in heraldry and should therefore be able to provide sound designs. The grantee on the other hand may have little or no knowledge of the subject and be possessed of limited artistic ability.

The mid-sixteenth century also witnessed a considerable increase in the number of grants of arms. Evidence is coming to light that the number of grants being made at the end of the sixteenth century may have been as many as ten times the number being granted at its beginning. Hawley's successor, William Hervey, Clarenceux King of Arms from 1557 to 1567, was responsible for approximately eighty grants a year. Many of these relate to the growing number of court officials and members of the professional and mercantile classes. A typical page of Hervey grants contains

Unusual grant of arms made to the Mines Royal Company in 1568. Untypical of Tudor heraldry, it is a precursor of later pictorial and landscape heraldry.
COLL. ARMS VINCENT 162 P 80

The industrious Robert Cooke, Clarenceux King of Arms, and his successors in that office, Richard Lee and William Camden, were more conservative in their taste than their earlier Tudor predecessors. The grant by Camden of the lamia crest as a pun to William and Simon Lambart in 1612 is therefore untypical. The scholarly Camden does not appear to have been interested in the innovative; he erroneously blazons the lamia as a 'manticore'.

COLL. ARMS ORIGINAL GRANT

twenty-three entries, including the Queen's physician, a skinner of London, a serjeant-at-law, an alderman of London, a Doctor of the Arches, a knight, a Londoner, a gentleman of unspecified location or occupation, a gentleman of Devon, a Londoner, a water bailiff of London, another Londoner, a gentleman of Warwickshire, a gentleman of Norfolk, another of unspecified residence, another of Cornwall, two master cooks to the Queen, the Lord Mayor of London, the latter's wife, a gentleman of Kingston in Surrey and two goldsmiths of London. By 1584, the centenary of the first incorporation of the heralds and the foundation of the College of Arms, the simplification of heraldic design first seen under Hawley as a reaction to the Wriothesley/Benolt period had intensified. The heraldry of the time was largely the responsibility of the industrious Robert Cooke, Clarenceux King of Arms from 1567 to 1593.

William Segar, Garter King of Arms from 1604 to 1633, wrote of Cooke that he 'confirmed and gave Armes and Crests without number to base and unworthy persons for his private gaine onely without the knowledge of the Erle Marshall'. There was certainly much activity in Cooke's office in 1584. *Hare's Ordinary* lists twenty-five Cooke grants for that year. Of other undated grants from this same source, between fourteen and twenty-one are likely to have fallen within the same period, which suggests that Cooke was approaching something in the region of a new grant each week. However, this is misleading. There is every reason to suppose that Cooke accelerated the rate achieved by William Hervey. Although Cooke was accused of making nearly five hundred grants over thirty years, an analysis of late Tudor heraldry suggests that this figure is missing a nought and that the real number of Cooke grants was nearer five thousand, suggesting a figure of 150 new armorial bearings for 1584 alone.

Cooke's heraldry follows the style established by Hawley. He made full use of the ordinaries, usually leaving these plain. When departing from this it was usually to adopt the engrailed line. Other varied lines were generally avoided. Twelve examples of engrailing occur in one hundred consecutive grants made around 1584. Cooke then favoured combining these ordinaries with a single additional charge, repeated three times when used with a fess or chevron. Similarly when charging a cross or saltire five similar charges were used or four when a cross or saltire was placed between them. In only seven out of these same one hundred grants is a further additional charge to be found. Cooke's charges were essentially traditional: lions, lions' heads, faces and gambs (paws), boars' heads, mullets and escallops found particular favour.

Cooke's style of heraldry is neat and well composed, but arguably it remains somewhat dull. Gone is the exuberance of

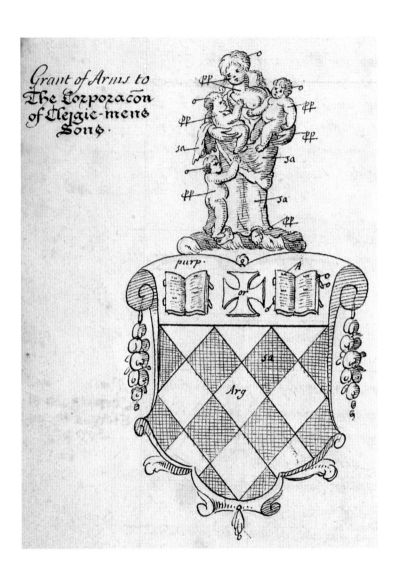

The armorial bearings of the Corporation of Clergymen's Sons, granted in 1684.
COLL ARMS GRANTS III P 250

early Tudor heraldry which, although frequently lacking balance and control in design, nonetheless possessed excitement and a sense of innovation. As with his arms, Cooke's crests relied heavily on traditional charges. In thirty consecutive Cooke crests granted in or about 1584 there were five eagles, four gryphons, two lions, two human arms, two heraldic tygers, two ermines, two talbots, one ounce, one cock, one stag, one cockatrice, one martlet, one bull, one swan, one ostrich, one dove, one boar and one fox. Such crests in a single tincture are then differenced in a simple way: either issuing from or collared with a coronet is a much preferred form of design. The more exotic creatures and monsters found a hundred years previously were generally ignored, and Cooke provided nothing new to replace them. It is possible that this conservatism reflects Cooke's own taste. On the other hand it may indicate a wider and popular sentiment that new heraldry should be traditional. This attitude was to become increasingly apparent during the next hundred years.

By 1684 the conservatism of heraldry was such that its survival seemed in question. Associated with the increasingly unpopular heralds' visitations, soon to be terminated with the final Visitation of London in 1687, heraldry appeared ill-suited to adapt to the changing times. On the one hand there was a failure to innovate which might otherwise have provided an outlet for creative heraldic design; on the other hand there was the apparent inability, perhaps excusable under the existing circumstances, to check the growing number of new men, the product of economic and social change, from quietly appropriating armorial bearings to which they had no entitlement. The number of grants made in 1684 was only eight. Of these one was to a corporate body, the Corporation of Clergymen's Sons, a charity set up for the relief of the widows and children of clergymen. A gloomy grant, made at a gloomy time in the history of heraldry, it is blazoned as *Lozengy Argent and Sable on a Chief Purpure a Cross Paty Or between two Books opened Argent the leaves cover and clasp Gold and for the crest the Efigies of Charitie standing on a Wreath of the Colours of the Field habited in a loose Garment Sable, her face, breast, hands and feet proper, her hair dishevelled Or, accompanied with three naked boys vis one on her dexter side and the others in her arms all proper and crined Gold.*

Of the seven remaining grants, one was for the wife of John Dugdale, Windsor Herald, and the others were for a doctor of physick from Norwich, the Recorder of the City of London, one of the chaplains-in-ordinary to the King, an ex-High Sheriff of Hertfordshire, an alderman and sometime mayor of Cambridge and a would-be gentleman from St Albans. The style of heraldic design of 1684 differs little from that of the late Tudor period. Only the pegasus crest to the Doctor of Physick provides a little interest among otherwise plain-lined ordinaries, lions, eagles, roses and other familiar and essentially conservative charges.

At the end of the seventeenth century the system whereby the heralds had carried out systematic surveys of all the counties of England and Wales ceased after more than 150 years. The termination of these visitations tended to restrict new grantees to the London area. Furthermore from 1676 it was laid down by the Earl Marshal that new grantees must either be holders of public office or able to produce two suitable references; these were somewhat discouraging requirements. The heralds themselves found heraldry unrewarding and occupied themselves with ceremonial matters and genealogy. Between December 1704 and December 1706 no new grants of armorial bearings were made, and this period can rightly be considered as the lowest point in the history of English heraldry. Sir John Vanbrugh was then Clarenceux King of Arms. As a gifted playwright and architect, it might be thought that he would have influenced the course of heraldry, but as a heraldic designer his influence was negligible.

By 1784 the position had improved. Forty new grants were made in that year. A number of these were based on earlier armorial bearings which had hitherto been used by the grantee without proper authority. Some families were at last becoming aware that the appropriation of the arms of another family of the same

The armorial bearings granted in 1784 to the brothers Charles and William Smith suggest that good composition and design were not always of importance in late eighteenth-century heraldry.

Coll. Arms Grants XV p 293

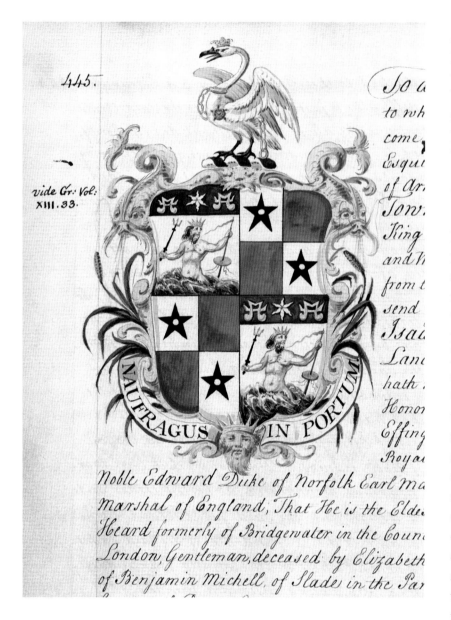

The armorial bearings granted in 1762 to Isaac Heard, Lancaster Herald and subsequently Garter King of Arms, showing Neptune rising from a natural stormy sea grasping the head of the mast of the ship in which Heard was shipwrecked.

COLL. ARMS GRANTS X P 445

surname, with whom they had no known connection, was not a proper way to behave and were therefore rectifying the position by having grants of armorial bearings in their own right.

In addition to new designs based on earlier heraldry, 1784 witnessed somewhat hesitant attempts to bring in fresh ideas. This was not always satisfactory and gave rise to such as the 1784 grant to Charles Smith, an officer in the Royal Artillery, and to his brother William Smith, captain in the East India Company. These arms show the use of dissimilar charges scattered with ordinaries and sub-ordinaries with little real sense of composition or design. The charges are obvious allusions to the careers of the Smith brothers, with a different crest for each. It is arguable that this choice of the obvious in the late eighteenth-century heraldry was too often made at the expense of the visual impact of heraldry.

The importance attached to the meaning of charges, regardless of their artistic effect, is perhaps demonstrated by several grants in which the choice of charge refers to a specific incident in the grantee's career. This type of heraldry found a staunch supporter in Sir Isaac Heard, Garter King of Arms from 1784 to 1822. Heard had been a midshipman when he was swept overboard and nearly drowned off the Guinea Coast in 1750. His subsequent grant of armorial bearings reflected this event. His

arms are blazoned as *Argent in base a Neptune with an Eastern Crown Or his Trident Sable headed Or issuing from a stormy Ocean the left hand grasping the head of a Ship's Mast appearing above the Waves as part of a Wreck proper on a Chief Azure the Arctic Polar Star of the first between two Water Bougets of the second.* Heard's attachment to historical episodes found an outlet in the heraldry of the Napoleonic period, when his grants not only included medallions and trophies of war but whole landscape scenes of broken ships and blasted forts. This era of landscape heraldry was to last into the middle of the nineteenth century, thereafter lingering on in corporate heraldry, particularly with overseas territories and local authorities.

Twentieth-century heralds are only too familiar with the submission of ideas for design which might be more appropriate for tourism advertisements. They have ranged from a representation of a local church or temple to whole landscapes complete with mountain, forest and the farmer working in a valley, and seascapes of rocky islands with fishing boats and assorted seabirds in cloudy

Above left: The armorial bearings granted to Hugh Gough in 1816 showing the breached battlements of Tarisa and the Badge of the Order of Charles III. Badges, medals and landscape heraldry were typical of the Heard period.
Coll. Arms Grants XXIX p 310

Above right: Crest granted to John Cameron in 1815 showing a Highlander of the 92nd Regiment waist-deep in water, alluding to the crossing of the River Gave de Mouline at Arriverete on 17 February 1814.
Coll. Arms Grants XXIX p 383

The supporters of Sir Charles William Stewart, later Marquess of Londonderry, exemplify heraldry's preoccupation with the Napoleonic Wars; painted in 1813.
COLL. ARMS BATH BOOK VII P 21

skies. This is generally accepted as a debasement of heraldry. Perhaps it was an inevitable experiment which at least demonstrates that heraldry is never static and is prepared to entertain new ideas. However, it did allow for an understanding of why a particular design was chosen; nothing is clearer than a pictorial representation of a landscape.

It is also regrettable that the practice of reciting events, which dictated the choice of charges, was discontinued, leaving the observer of heraldic design to guess as to the reasoning behind it.

This loss was more than compensated for by the refreshing developments which took place in heraldic design in the second half of the nineteenth century when the number of grantees had more than doubled the corresponding number one hundred years previously. Of these grantees a modest number were impersonal, and these marked the beginning of a resurgence in corporate heraldry. An analysis of grants in 1884 reveals grants to the Borough of Harrogate, the Borough of Ramsgate and the newly constituted Diocese of Southwell. Of the personal grants in the same year there were supporters for three new peers, including those of Lord Tennyson: *Two Leopards guardant Gules Ducally Crowned and semy of Fleurs-de-lis Gold*. There was also the grant of supporters by Royal Licence to a Baronet, Sir Henry William Dashwood: *Two male Griffins Argent gorged with a Collar flory counter flory*. This last grant exemplifies something of a new spirit in heraldry, with the reintroduction of a fifteenth-century heraldic monster so untypical of the conservative heraldry of the intervening centuries.

The grants of 1884 also include that to Sophie Felicite de Rodes. Grants to women have never been numerous, but they have been consistent and in the late twentieth century they are beginning to take an increasing proportion of the whole. It is to be hoped that recent rulings of the kings of arms in respect of women will do much to encourage this trend. Future historians of heraldry may be able to point to the late twentieth century as the period when women began to play a major part in heraldic design.

Military figures and the natives of conquered territories continued to feature prominently in nineteenth-century designs, particularly with supporters. Sir Henry Pottinger's supporters, granted in 1845, feature a Chinese mandarin and a Sindian foot soldier.
COLL. ARMS GRANTS XLVIII P 10

Arms on a lozenge for an unmarried woman granted to Catherine Bingham in 1890, showing a simplicity and distinctiveness in design that was characteristic of much late nineteenth-century heraldry.
COLL. ARMS GRANTS LXV P 186

The heraldry of 1884 shows no attempt to introduce new charges. Even the unusual, such as the snail, cameleopard and the Dashwood male gryphons, were reintroductions rather than creatures making their first appearance in heraldry. The lion accounts for fifteen crests out of a total of eighty-two, the human arm for ten, the stag for six and the eagle for five, showing that long-used charges were still preferred.

Nonetheless, in contrast to 1784, the heraldry of the late nineteenth century is often refreshing. It manifests a new and frequently successful approach to design that can be traced back to Sir Charles Young, Garter King of Arms from 1842 to 1869. Young clearly had an interest in design, as it is recorded of him that 'as Garter he made unnecessary alterations in almost every sketch submitted to him and that he gave better coats to his own clients than to those of other officers'. His successor, Sir Albert Woods, Garter King of Arms from 1869 to 1904, has a reputation as a deplorable armorist. He often said that he was determined that any grants of armorial bearings made during his gartership should mark a period of history, that Victorian grants must be Victorian and that no nineteenth-century grantee could expect a simple coat. However, analysis of the grants made during this period does not reveal any marked difference between the Young and Woods years. The period was rich in innovation. Segmented heraldry, that is to say, the placing of different and frequently discordant charges above and below fess or chevron, continued; but it seems there was some effort to discard it. Varied lines were now favoured and covered the more unusual forms, such as flory, counter flory, dovetailed and rayonny. Ordinaries were frequently cotised; crosses were parted and fretted, made formy or botony; and there was a liberal use of gouttes, ermine spots and party divisions frequently counterchanged.

By the end of the nineteenth century it is also clear that the traditional positioning of charges was beginning to break down. No longer was it necessary to place three charges on a bend, fess or chevron. In 1884, for example, two greyhounds are courant on a bend and five horseshoes are charged on a chevron. A fess is set between two talbots' heads and there is a cross-couped charged with four bombs all between four anchors; the heraldry of earlier centuries would have used three talbots' heads, two above the fess and one below, and five bombs.

This approach to heraldic design favoured by Sir Charles Young was continued by his successors until the mid-twentieth century. Names like Sir Alfred Scott-Gatty, Sir Henry Farnham Burke and Charles Athill should be given credit for designing neat and interesting armorial bearings with none of the segmented clutter with which this period is too often credited. Curiously the traditional furs like vair and ermine, together with the varied lines, which proved popular in the nineteenth century, witnessed a decline, and there remained a reluctance to move beyond such

The armorial bearings granted in 1891 to Charles Harold Athill, Richmond Herald and subsequently Clarenceux King of Arms. Athill was one of the more notable designers of the late nineteenth century and his own arms and crest reflect his personal taste. Both are simple but retain lively interest by double cotising the chevron in the arms and interlacing the annulets and feathers in the crest.
COLL. ARMS GRANTS LXVI P 84

overused charges as lion, stag and birds of prey. Since any component part of the armorial achievement must be distinct from those already granted, it is to be hoped that the heralds will not shrink from bringing in new ideas and new charges and not rest content with rearranging the old. Any emphasis on flora and fauna and monsters is appropriate; man-made objects in heraldic design are not always to be encouraged, however. Heraldry is timeless and passes from generation to generation, and the inanimate all too often becomes outdated.

An analysis of grants of arms made in 1984, the quincentennial year of the foundation of the College of Arms, shows that the number of grantees had risen to 191, a figure which approximates to the number being granted today. The year 1906 saw the revival of the badge; and its use and development is now a characteristic of twentieth-century heraldry. There were no known grants of badges between the sixteenth century and 1906; but today the majority of grants includes a badge.

The reappearance of the badge has been a major factor influencing the design of arms where styles have become increasingly diverse and ingenious. As the badge is free-standing and not enclosed within the restricted area of the shield, it has encouraged the combining of charges to provide a single device which has then been introduced into the arms. Typical examples of this are fleur-de-lis with the petals terminating in animal heads or with the

Above: Badge granted to Sir James Horlick in 1915, showing the badge free-standing and also in the heraldic standard. With the revival of badges in 1906, objects were combined to provide a single device. Many were designed around a central point, allowing for the component parts to point outwards in different directions. Both these factors have in turn influenced the designing of arms in the twentieth century.
COLLEGE OF ARMS MS STANDARDS I P 143.

Right: The combination of scallop and trident creates a badge-like formation which is used as a single device in the arms of Wooster, granted in 1990.
COLL. ARMS GRANTS CLVI P 154.

Opposite page: Ivy leaves pointing outwards in the arms of Kydd, granted 1976. Badge designs stimulated a realisation that charges need not always point upwards.
COLL. ARMS GRANTS CXXXIX P 18

outer petals extending into wings; a harp terminating in a stag's head; martlets flying through coronets; pickaxes enfiling mullets; and a variety of charges encircled by annulets, frequently treated with a compound outer edge such as embattled, flory or potency. The free-standing nature of the badge has demanded its design as an isolated entity. This means that badges are often circular or symmetrical in form, which has encouraged an alignment of charges so that they point inwards or outwards from the centre. Heraldry is now rich in examples of animals facing each other or passant in opposite directions. Similarly flora and inanimate objects have stalks or apexes pointing inwards or outwards.

A more flexible attitude to heraldic design in the late twentieth century has made itself apparent in other ways, particularly with the wider use of the geometric formations of the shield. For example, the flaunch, the semi-circular formation issuing from the side of the shield, is now popular, and even the previously rare pall has received long overdue

Occupations are represented by:

Top left: Reversed chevronels combined with crescents and roundels represent bullying hockey sticks.
CORNOCK, 1989

Top right: Vary potenty field provides a series of black camera formations pointing at three castles for photography.
BOWEN-BRAVERY, 1985

Bottom left: Papillonny field suggests seats in an auditorium over which golden sound spreads, for a musician.
ROSS-RUSSELL, 1987

Bottom right: A blue field charged with three engrailed piles charged in turn with three blue inverted piles suggests coral and when combined with angel fish makes an allusion to snorkelling in tropical climes.
MORTON, 1984
DRAWINGS: HENRIETTA WEBB, BASED ON COLL. ARMS MSS

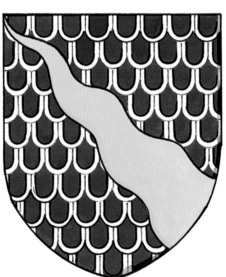

The use of traditional fields and geometric formations can be arranged to create simple yet distinctive heraldry alluding to leisure pursuits of grantees.

attention. There is little doubt that the freedom of design in modern heraldry and the rearranging of traditional charges have been to the disadvantage of searching for new. The principal exception to this is the flora and fauna from overseas, some of which has now become well established. The maple leaf and the wattle of Australia are good examples of this, as are the lyre bird and the Australian magpie or piping shrike. All were absent in 1984, but are now familiar charges. It is arguable that they are following the lion, stag and birds of prey into the category of the overused.

Occupations are represented by :

Top left: A red orle conjoined with a red pallet represent supermarket walkways and also make a 'T' and 'O' formation. The two windows or interstices are charged with cloves taken from the Company of Grocers.
TESCO STORES LTD 1979

Top right: Bars conjoined with fracted annulets enclosing roundels give a ball and socket formation as an allusion to arthritis.
GRAY, 1989

Bottom left: Conjoined barrulets and pallets suggest prison bars. These are broken into by conjoining with annulets through which light shines in the form of estoiles. The whole is an allusion to furthering the cause of hospital treatment for prisoners.
REED, 1997

Bottom right: A flaunch formation conjoined with a bar suggests the United Kingdom joined to Continental Europe, the blue and white representing the Channel and its shore; the Channel Tunnel is thus represented.
PENNOCK, 1991
DRAWINGS: HENRIETTA WEBB, BASED ON COLL. ARMS MSS

New inanimate charges are rare. Analysis of the grants of armorial bearings made between 1982 and 1983 reveals a cream-skimmer, a pair of swivels and the prow of a Viking ship; the following year produced a *ko* (a Maori digging stick), and a *koruru* (a Maori carved head), a tuning cone and a reed-hook. Chemical symbols become evident with the DNA chain, the benzene ring and a conventional representation of the neutron and another of the atom. The benzene ring in particular will become an increasingly popular heraldic charge with its simple and distinctive formation.

Traditional geometric formations combined with simple charges to provide punning arms:

Top left: A blue fret charged with a gold fret, thus 'deux' (two) frets.
DEFRATES, 1990

Top right: Saltires conjoined to a pallet suggest poles charged with two suns.
POLSTON, 1993

Bottom left: A fess coronetty is an allusion to a ducal coronet.
DUKE, 1995

Bottom right: A pallet conjoined to a saltire and a voided hexagon allude to the cells of a honeycomb, the fleur-de-lis representing France.
FRANKCOM, 1985
DRAWINGS: HENRIETTA WEBB, BASED ON COLL. ARMS MSS

Late twentieth-century heraldry frequently reflects the occupation or career of the grantee or his ancestors. The pun is still apparent, and cognate heraldry is widely used, particularly when it takes charges from the arms of the county or school with which a grantee has been associated. Leisure pursuits have also produced a new and important source of design. Here the basic geometric formations of traditional heraldry can be rearranged in many forms, using partition lines to suggest photography, snorkelling, mountaineering, backgammon, the theatre, sailing, gardening and much else. Leisure has become a major ingredient in twentieth-century heraldic design.

Critical comments on heraldic design are often levelled against the herald. Most heralds have had the experience of awaking in the morning to find comments on their efforts splashed across the national or local press. In some instances the herald concerned may well deserve the criticism; but the fault may often lie with the grantee. In any design of new armorial bearings the wishes of the grantee must be taken into account. As the expert in heraldry, the herald should in most cases be able to direct the ideas and suggestions of the grantee towards a suitable and rewarding design. The means by which heralds arrive at this have probably altered very little since the fifteenth or sixteenth centuries. It therefore serves to describe the process as it operates today.

Initially an approach is made by the would-be grantee to the College of Arms or to an individual herald. The College's counterpart in Scotland is the Court of Lord Lyon. The first duty of the herald who receives the enquiry is to ensure that the grantee is eligible to petition for a grant of armorial bearings to be made by the kings of arms, who are empowered to grant only to 'eminent' men and women. In practice, eligibility depends upon holding a civil or military commission, a sound university degree or professional qualification, or having achieved some measure of distinction in a field beneficial to society as a whole. Similarly, grants of armorial bearings are made to corporate bodies which include local authorities, places of education, professional bodies as well as commercial companies which are leading in their particular field.

Once the formal petition has been accepted, the grantee is asked by the acting herald to submit ideas or allusions for a design. Although there is therefore an input from the grantee, the herald must ensure that any ideas are sufficiently distinctive from anything already on the register. Whilst it is right and proper that the grantee should be allowed to express any wishes, it is also the duty of the herald with his expertise as a designer to steer that grantee into obtaining an example of worthwhile heraldry. Individual allusions and charges are perhaps less important that the ultimate visual effect of the design. It is this emphasis on the art of heraldry which should ensure that it has a rich and creative future.

Glossary

Achievement: The full armorial bearings of an armiger, i.e. shield, crest, helm, wreath, mantling, motto and supporters

Addorsed: Placed back to back

Affronty: Facing the viewer

Appaumy: With the palm of the hand facing the viewer

Argent: White or silver

Armed: Toothed, tusked, horned or clawed

Armiger: One who is entitled to armorial bearings

Attired: Antlered, as with stags

Augmentation: An additional charge granted as a mark of honour

Azure: Blue

Bar: A horizontal band, a diminutive of the fess

Barbed: Having small leaves appearing between the petals of an open rose; also with a sharp head as with an arrow

Barry: An even series of horizontal bands

Baton: A bend couped or cut off at both ends

Bend: A diagonal band running from the dexter chief to the sinister base

Bendlet: A diminutive of the bend

Bendy: An even series of bends

Bezant: A gold roundel

Billet: A rectangle

Blazon: The technical language describing armorial bearings

Bleu celeste: Sky blue

Bordure: A border

Caboshed: An animal's head affronty without any neck

Cadency marks: Non-obligatory small devices added to distinguish junior members of a family

Canton: A square in one of the upper corners of the arms

Checky/chequy: Composed of small adjoining squares

Chevron: A broad inverted V

Chevronel: A diminutive of the chevron

Chevronny: An even series of chevronels

Chief: A broad horizontal band at the top of the shield

Close: Wings folded

Colours: The principal colours are azure (blue), gules (red), sable (black), and vert (green). The less frequently used colours are bleu celeste (sky blue), purpure (purple), murrey (dark red) and tenne (orange). Murrey and tenne are sometimes termed 'stains'.

Combatant: Two rampant creatures facing each other

Compartment: A grassy mount or solid base on which supporters stand

Company/gobony: A single row of squares of alternate tinctures

Glossary

Cotise: The smallest diminutive of the bend, fess, cross, chevron etc. and borne on either side of the same

Couchant: A creature lying down with its head held up

Counterchanged: A field divided between two different tinctures and having charges superimposed with these tinctures reversed

Couped: Cut off cleanly at the base

Courant: Running

Coward: With tail between the legs

Crosslet: A cross with each limb crossed again

Cruisily: Strewn with crosslets

Dancetty zigzag: Said of a two-sided charge such as a fess with offset indentations on each side so that it 'dances'. Sometimes but erroneously used as a shallow variety of indented.

Dexter: The right side. When applied to a shield it refers to that part which would be on the right side of the bearer and thus the left side as viewed from the front.

Diapering: Decorative patterning on uncharged areas of the shield executed in the same tincture

Dimidiation: The cutting of two coats of arms in half and placing them together to form a single shield. Also applied to two charges treated in the same way.

Displayed: Wings outstretched and sweeping upwards

Dormant: Sleeping

Doubled: Lined when applied to mantling

Emanchy: A zigzag line of partition with acute angles

Embowed: Bent at the elbow

Embrued: Blooded at the point

Enfile: To thread

Engrailed: Indented in a series of curves, points outwards

Ensigned: Having another charge placed above

Erased: Jaggedly cut or torn off at the base

Ermine: White with black ermine spots

Ermines: Black with white ermine spots

Erminois: Gold with black ermine spots

Escutcheon: A small shield. When a blank escutcheon is charged on arms it indicates a married woman, the arms being her own.

Fess: A broad horizontal band running across the centre of the shield

Field: The basic surface of the shield on which the charges are placed

Fimbriated: Edged

Fitchy: Terminating in a point, usually applied to the lower limb of a cross

Flaunch: A convex segment issuing from the side of the shield

Flory: Terminating in fleur-de-lis

Formy: Splayed, usually applied to the limb of a cross

Forcene: Rearing up when applied to horses

Fountain: A roundel composed of wavy bars in white and blue

Fourchy: Forked, normally applied to the tails of animals

Fret: A mascle interlaced with a saltire

Fructed: A tree or plant bearing fruit

Fusil: An elongated lozenge

Gamb: A paw

Gorged: Collared

Goutte: A droplet

Guardant: An animal with body in profile and head facing the viewer

Gules: Red

Gutty: Strewn with gouttes

Gyronny: A series of division lines emanating from a central point to create triangular pieces or gyrons

Hatching: A system for identifying tinctures in monochrome by a series of dots and lines

Hauriant: Placed vertically with head upwards, applied to fish

Hurt: A blue roundel

Impale: To place two coats of arms side by side on a single shield for husband and wife or for office and office-holder

Indented: A zigzag line of partition; when applied to a charge with two sides such as a fess the indentations are opposite each other

Invected: A line of partition with a series of curves, points inwards

Issuant: Issuing from

Jessant de lis: With a fleur-de-lis issuing from an object, usually applied to an animal's head

Label: A narrow horizontal strip across the top of the shield with three or five tags pendant from it, usually found as a mark of cadency for the eldest son during his father's lifetime

Langued: Tongued

Lodged: Deer when couchant (i.e. lying down with head up)

Lozenge: A diamond shape. When a small blank lozenge is charged on a shield it denotes the arms of a married woman, the arms being those of her husband.

Mantling: The stylised cloak or mantle hanging from the helm

Marshal: To combine coats of arms on a single shield

Mascle: A voided diamond shape. When a single small mascle is found on a shield it denotes a divorced woman.

Metals: Or (gold) and argent (white or silver)

Moline: Terminating in two outward-curving points

Murrey: Dark red

Naiant: Swimming horizontally

Nebuly: A wavy division line where the waves take the form of nodules

Nowed: Tied in the form of a knot when applied to snakes or the tails of animals

Nowy: A cross with a large circular centre

Ogress: A black roundel or pellet

Or: Gold or yellow

Ordinary: Any one of the major geometrical charges. Also a systematic collection of armorials arranged according to the charges therein.

Orle: A band following the outline of the shield but set away from the edge

Pairle: A division in the form of a Y

Pale: A vertical band running down the centre of the shield

Pall: A Y shape

Pallet: A narrow vertical band, a diminutive of the pale

Paly: Divided into an equal series of vertical bands

Passant: Walking on all fours in profile

Paty: Splayed and flory formation, usually applied to the limbs of a cross

Pean: Black with gold ermine spots

Glossary

Pellet: A black roundel or ogress

Pile: A triangular shape issuing from the top, base or sides of the shield

Plate: A white roundel

Pomme: A green roundel

Potent: Crossed at the end, like the head of a crutch

Proper: In natural colours

Purpure: Purple

Quadrate: A cross with an enlarged square centre

Quarter: To divide the shield into four or more pieces of equal size

Queue: The tail of a creature

Rampant: Prancing, a creature standing erect on one hind leg

Reguardant: Looking backwards over the shoulder

Roundel: A circular disk

Sable: Black

Salient: Leaping with both hind legs lowered

Saltire: A cross in the form of an X

Segreant: Rampant when applied to gryphons

Sejant: Sitting

Semy: Strewn or powdered

Sinister: The left hand side as opposed to the right (dexter)

Slipped: Stalked

Statant: Standing

Tenne: Orange

Tinctures: The metals, colours and furs

Torse: The crest wreath, normally depicted with six visible twists

Torteau: A red roundel

Tressure: A diminutive of the orle

Trick: To indicate tinctures in uncoloured armorial bearings by written abbreviations

Trippant: Passant when applied to deer

Undy: Wavy

Urinant: Placed vertically with head downwards, applied to fish

Vair: Back and belly squirrel skins stitched together

Vert: Green

Voided: With the centre removed, following the outline of the charge

Volant: Flying

Bibliography

A New Dictionary of Heraldry, edited by Stephen Friar, Alphabooks Ltd (A. & C. Black, 1987)

Boutell's Heraldry, revised by J.P. Brook-Little, Norroy & Ulster King of Arms (Frederick Warne & Co. Ltd, 1983)

Chenciner, Robert, *The Bayeux Tapestry* (paper delivered at the Oxford Food Symposium, 1990)

Costello, Peter, *The Magic Zoo* (Sphere Books, 1979)

Dennys, Rodney, *The Heraldic Imagination* (Barrie and Jenkins, 1975)

Fox-Davies, A.C.A., revised by J.P. Brooke-Little, *A Complete Guide to Heraldry* (Orbis, 1985)

George, Wilma, and Brinston Yup, *The Naming of the Beasts* (Duckworth, 1991)

George, Wilma, *Animals and Maps* (Secker and Warburg, 1969)

Payne, Ann, *Mediaeval Beasts* (The British Library, 1990)

Quarterly Magazine, The Heraldry Society

Scott Giles, Wilfred, Fitzalan Pursuivant Extraordinary, *The Romance of Heraldry* (J.M. Dent & Sons Ltd, 1967)

The Coat of Arms, edited by J.P. Brooke-Little

Wagner, Sir Anthony, KCVO, Garter King of Arms, *Heralds of England* (HMSO, 1967)

Woodcock, Thomas, and John Martin Robinson, *The Oxford Guide to Heraldry* (Oxford University Press, 1988)

Index